"I was challenged by this book in the best wa[...] [...] heart to Christ's. Amy DiMarcangelo remin[...] [...] deeds and calling of my Savior. That alone was so encouraging. But then she showed me how to go and do likewise in my own life and context. This book is both worshipful and practical. It can feel overwhelming to see the needs of the world and not know how to engage. But I ended the book with both the peace of my sovereign Savior and the urgency of his call to go. If you want to follow in the footsteps of Jesus, start here."

**Jen Oshman**, author, *Enough about Me* and *Cultural Counterfeits*; Podcaster, *All Things*

"Too often Christians feel like they have to choose between the Great Commission and the Great Commandment, between compassion and conviction. Scripture, however, doesn't allow us to do that. Amy DiMarcangelo walks readers through the pages of Scripture, joyfully inviting them to engage in Christ's mission to redeem and restore. If you love Jesus and want to follow him into a lost and dying world, you'll want to pick up this book."

**Daniel Darling**, Director, The Land Center for Cultural Engagement; Columnist, *WORLD*; author, *The Dignity Revolution*; *The Characters of Christmas*; and *Agents of Grace*

"I've never read a book that speaks to mission quite the way Amy Di-Marcangelo's does. This is a missions book for ordinary folk—nonheroic Christians who are faithful but need fresh lights pointing in new directions. DiMarcangelo helps us by navigating a wise and compelling course—not veering into guilt motivation, but at the same time not letting us comfortable Christians applaud but stay out of the game. She balances 'go take risks' and 'stay and support well,' physical needs and spiritual needs, justice and mercy, compassion and wisdom. DiMarcangelo's writing and life are driven by an infectious passion to glorify Jesus in tangible and self-denying ways. It's a passion that always circles back to biblical truth and gospel focus. DiMarcangelo speaks challenge to my comfort, faith to my fears, and tasks to my hands. Let her do the same for you."

**Andy Farmer**, pastor; author, *Ordinary Greatness: A Life of Elias Boudinot*

"*Go and Do Likewise* is a compelling call to ordinary Christians—all Christians—to join the mission of gospel-fueled mercy and justice. With great wisdom and humility, Amy DiMarcangelo challenges and inspires readers with a thoroughly biblical, Christ-exalting view of missional living. This book is equal parts theological and practical. It will do more than encourage and convict you; it will inform and equip you. Most of it all, it will lead you to a deeper love of Jesus and a greater love of those he loves. *Go and Do Likewise* has gained a permanent place on my shelf, and I plan to reread it—and reorient my heart to its message—on a regular basis."

**Jamie Finn**, author, *Foster the Family*

*Go and Do Likewise*

# GO AND DO LIKEWISE

A CALL TO FOLLOW JESUS IN A LIFE OF MERCY AND MISSION

## AMY DiMARCANGELO

CROSSWAY®

WHEATON, ILLINOIS

**Library of Congress Cataloging-in-Publication Data**

Names: DiMarcangelo, Amy, 1988– author.
Title: Go and do likewise : a call to follow Jesus in a life of mercy and mission / by Amy DiMarcangelo.
Description: Wheaton, Illinois : Crossway, 2023. | Includes bibliographical references and index. |
    Summary: "Explains how ordinary Christians can demonstrate God's compassion, uncovering practical
    ways to extend mercy to the vulnerable and suffering in everyday life"—Provided by publisher.
Identifiers: LCCN 2023001082 (print) | LCCN 2023001083 (ebook) | ISBN 9781433588068 (trade
    paperback) | ISBN 9781433588075 (pdf) | ISBN 9781433588099 (epub)
Subjects: LCSH: Compassion—Religious aspects—Christianity.
Classification: LCC BV4647.S9 D56 2023 (print) | LCC BV4647.S9 (ebook) | DDC 205/.677—dc23/
    eng/20230417
LC record available at https://lccn.loc.gov/2023001082

Crossway is a publishing ministry of Good News Publishers.

| VP | | 32 | 31 | 30 | 29 | 28 | 27 | 26 | 25 | 24 | 23 |
|----|----|----|----|----|----|----|----|----|----|----|----|
| 15 | 14 | 13 | 12 | 11 | 10 | 9 | 8 | 7 | 6 | 5 | 4 | 3 | 2 | 1 |

*To the women who cared for our daughter until we could—*
*words aren't sufficient to express my gratitude for you.*

# Contents

# Introduction

INDIA IS A BEAUTIFUL COUNTRY. But driving past the sprawling slums of Mumbai does something to a person. I first saw them when I was fifteen, and I haven't forgotten them since.

My dad was teaching at a pastors' conference in India, and knowing my desire to serve there in the future, he invited me to join him. Our trip was only two weeks long, but it changed my life. I was so moved by the ministry being done by my Indian brothers and sisters in Christ. Planting churches in remote villages, offering quality education to impoverished kids, caring for orphans, comforting the persecuted, sending young women to nursing school, providing jobs for people who'd been marginalized because of their disabilities—it seemed they had a hand in every part of serving their communities. Faced with overwhelming physical and spiritual need, this ministry faithfully demonstrated the good news of Jesus Christ in both word and deed. It was something I wanted to be a part of, and I dreamed about life and ministry there.

When I returned home, it was difficult to wrestle with the culture shock. Hitting me like an avalanche, I was suddenly aware of all the blessings I experienced that other people didn't. Who was I to have a dresser packed to the brim, when so many live in tattered clothes? Who was I to have plans for college, when so many women around the world had no access to education? Who was I to live with my family in the suburbs, when so many families had been torn apart because of wars and violence? God used that trip to stir me to live more generously and find ways to serve those in need, but I also began to struggle with nagging guilt about the "goodness" of my life.

I still wrestle with it today. Whether hearing a story from one of my refugee friends, or reading one of those convicting, inspiring, hard-but-good books (I'm looking at you, David Platt!), the struggle hits me afresh.

*Who am I to have this life? How can I be radically generous, compassionate, and servant-hearted when I live among the middle class? What does it look like to follow Jesus in his mercy-filled mission?*

As I've wrestled through this, I've had to grapple with my own misunderstanding of radical faithfulness to the mission. It's not some nebulous pursuit only in derelict cities or developing countries. It's here. It's now. God has equipped all of us to be doers of mercy in different ways and in different places. There are biblical mandates we're all called to obey, but there's no one-size-fits-all answer about how to obey them. The principles of God's word are timeless, applicable to every person in every season in every situation and in every place.

Just like the saints who have gone before us, we live among sinful people in need of forgiveness, broken people in need of healing, afflicted people in need of comfort. Sin and suffering sear the earth and would relegate us all to damnation and despair if not for the gospel of Jesus Christ. He came to redeem fallen people and to restore a fallen world. And he's chosen to work through those in the church—instruments of his very body—as a means of this restoration. He's chosen to work through *us*.

I want this book to leave each of you excited and equipped to become a doer of mercy as you take part in God's mission to the world. He doesn't need any of us to accomplish his good work—which is as humbling as it is relieving—but he graciously invites each of us to participate in it. A. W. Tozer explains it this way:

> Let us not imagine that the truth of the divine self-sufficiency will paralyze Christian activity. Rather it will stimulate all holy endeavor. The truth, while a needed rebuke to human self-confidence, will when viewed in its Biblical perspective lift from our minds the exhausting load of mortality and encourage us to take the easy yoke of Christ and spend ourselves in Spirit-inspired toil for the honor of God and the good of mankind. For the blessed news is that the God who needs no one has in sovereign condescension stooped to work by and in and through His obedient children.[1]

Brothers and sisters, God doesn't need our help—yet he chooses to work through us. This is a privilege. A blessed calling. An exciting endeavor. Without bearing the crushing weight of responsibility to heal a broken world, we have the joy of partnering in God's redemptive work. Most of us won't do this by becoming full-time missionaries or by founding charitable organizations. Most of us

1 A. W. Tozer, *The Knowledge of the Holy* (New York: HarperCollins, 1961), 36.

will live unremarkable and ordinary lives. But our ordinary lives can be just as devoted to his kingdom.

This book is for those of you who feel overwhelmed by the suffering you see and care passionately about the oppressed and impoverished but feel frustrated that you don't know how to respond. It's also for those of you who—whether intentionally or unintentionally—live blissfully unaware of such needs.

It's for those of you who dream of glamorous ways to serve the Lord and need vision for the ministry found in the mundane. It's also for those of you who are too preoccupied with your daily lives to remember the broader mission of God's redemptive work.

It's for those of you who had happy childhoods, loving families, and financial security and are uniquely positioned to use those advantages to bless those in need. It's also for those of you who grew up in broken homes, have experienced poverty and oppression, and are uniquely positioned to do for others what you wish had been done for you.

No matter where you come from or where you are, know this: God has put you where you are for a reason—to live as an extension of *his* loving compassion and mercy in a suffering world.

# 1

# God's Story Shapes
# Our Perspective

I'M AN AVID READER and love a good story. The problem is, I read multiple books at once and have a terrible memory. As you'd imagine, this can lead to a bit of confusion. Sometimes I'll forget where I am in a story arc and mix up characters. If I've taken too long of a break between one book and another, I have to skim the chapters I've already read just to remember major plotlines. No matter how good a story is, we won't enjoy it if we forget where we are.

This also applies to life. God has written—and is writing—a beautiful story of redemption, but we can forget where it is and our place in it. And when we overlook major plot points in Scripture, we're left confused, aimless, or hopeless about our present age. We need a perspective shift. If we want to be faithful doers of mercy, we need to get ourselves oriented in God's story of redemption.

## The Grand Narrative

In the beginning, God created a beautiful world and supplied everything it needed to thrive. He made Adam and Eve to enjoy communion with him and each other. The garden of Eden was fruitful and flourishing, and the cultural mandate to steward the earth wasn't one of drudgery, but delight. Relationships were good. Work was good. Everything was good. That was the setup—from the start, God designed us for abundance, joy, and love.

Then came the conflict. A wicked serpent tempted Adam and Eve to disobey their generous Creator. When they chose to rebel, evil stained the world. What was once perfect became broken, shattered into an array of sin and suffering. But in the rubble, God revealed a glimmer of hope. Through Eve's offspring, he would send someone to crush the head of the serpent (Gen. 3:15).

We don't know much at first. But as the story develops, God reveals more about the promised one and all he would accomplish. Through the prophets and the covenants and the history of the Old Testament, we get glimpses of what was to come. Each story of deliverance, redemption, and atonement ultimately points forward to Jesus—the serpent crusher. The deliverer from bondage. The one who would reign as a king and be a blessing to all nations. And yet there was a confounding detail often misunderstood—this victory would happen through suffering.

Then we approach the climax. Jesus came to earth as the God-man. He lived in perfect obedience and embodied love, righteousness, justice, and mercy. He showed the world what the Father is like and how man is called to live. He succeeded where Adam failed. And through many miracles, he revealed his power to reverse the curse. He was the one who would heal the shattered world.

But then came a major plot twist: he *died*.

The promised one died.

The person supposed to restore all things died.

Don't let your familiarity with the story make it lose its impact.

The *hero* was rejected and condemned and died.

And yet somehow—in a subversive turn only God could design—Christ's death was how he secured his victory. As he was high and lifted up on the cross, he was establishing himself as King. All along, he planned to crush the head of the serpent by being crushed for us. And when he rose three days later, he proved his power over sin and death. The promised victory was won. He gave us a hope and a future.

But no story ends at the climax. There's a falling action and only *after* that, a conclusion. Jesus won, but we're still awaiting the final resolution. We're in the in-between, the already not yet part of the kingdom. Jesus is making all things new, and someday he will return to complete that work. His *atoning* work for sins is finished, but his *redemptive* work to restore his kingdom isn't. Victory is certain, but there is still sin and suffering, brokenness and pain.

What's the relevance of all this? Why skim the redemptive story in a book about mercy? It's because it deeply shapes how we think and feel and live. We must know God's grand narrative in order to understand our place in the plotline. We need to understand what our Savior *did* and what he's *doing*. We need to remember how the world was *originally* designed to see how far it has fallen. This perspective shows us what needs to be redeemed in the first place. It helps us recognize what's gone amiss so that we can play a part in its restoration.

We live in the already-not-yet. Jesus won, but the world is still reeling in pain, groaning for him to make it new. As we follow Christ our King, we're called to take part in his work of healing the world.

## Know Your Setting

Knowing our place in the context of the biblical story of redemption also helps us make sense of our cultural context. We live in a particular time and place, where there are particular ways to seek God's kingdom. When we pray, "Your kingdom come, your will be done, on earth as it is in heaven," we have a part to play. As the body of Christ, we move in conjunction with him to restore what sin has broken.

This restorative work has looked different throughout history. Sociologist and historian Rodney Stark argues that one of the main reasons for explosive growth in the early church was that Christians showed mercy to the suffering. During two devastating plagues, Christians throughout the Roman Empire risked their lives to care for the sick—both those in and outside the household of faith:

> What went on during the epidemics was only an intensification of what went on every day among Christians. . . . Indeed, the impact of Christian mercy was so evident that in the fourth century when the emperor Julian attempted to restore paganism, he exhorted the pagan priesthood to compete with the Christian charities. In a letter to the high priest of Galatia, Julian urged the distribution of grain and wine to the poor,

noting that "the impious Galileans [Christians], in addition to their own, support ours."[1]

In the twelfth and thirteenth centuries, Christians across Europe established leper houses and hospitals to care for the poor and sick.[2] In eighteenth-century India, Pandita Ramabai founded Mukti Mission, a Christian charity devoted to aiding destitute girls, widows, and temple prostitutes.[3] The church has a long and rich history of caring for the vulnerable, with Christians establishing many of the first hospitals and orphanages and social programs. The needs are different now, as are our means to meet them. So it's important to consider our current setting. How is God moving *now*? What has he called us to do *now*? When the church faithfully stands on the front lines to care for those in need, it strengthens our witness. When we don't, it damages it.

It's easier to lament suffering in bygone ages than grieve it today. We denounce past atrocities—and those who ignored them—without seeing our own propensity to do the same. This is the danger of generational pride, where we judge previous generations for their errors but are blind to our own. Blatant expressions of wickedness in history are easy to identify. Chattel slavery was barbaric. The Holocaust, unimaginable. The abuse of the mentally ill in early asylums, criminal. All of it, unjustifiable. But it's important for us to understand how each of these historic evils happened through

---

1   Rodney Stark, *The Triumph of Christianity: How the Jesus Movement Became the World's Largest Religion* (New York: HarperOne, 2011), 114–19.

2   Adam J. Davis, "The Charitable Revolution," ed. Chris R. Armstrong, *Christian History* 101 (2011), https://christianhistoryinstitute.org/.

3   Shirley Ray Redmond, *Courageous World Changers* (Eugene, OR: Harvest, 2020), 10.

the compounding nature of sin. Subtle prejudices and small exploitations grew into something monstrous. That's just how sin works. It's sinister, blinding, and deceiving us as it grows and devours. Satan doesn't care if we condemn sins of the past so long as we ignore the sins of the present. This is why it's so important for us—as individuals and local churches—to honestly and humbly engage hard questions, like: *Whose exploitation are we blind to? Are there any ways we've been complicit in the mistreatment of others? How might future generations look back on the church today, grieved by our apathy to evil?* God is faithful from generation to generation. He will help us walk in both repentance and righteousness and give us wisdom to engage the evils of our present day.

It's uncomfortable though. We don't *want* to live in a bubble, and yet many of us do just that. Life is already painful, and we're naturally self-focused. When we're consumed only with our own struggles, our own heartaches, and our own desires, we'll be blind to the hurting neighbors God puts in our path. We can't be doers of mercy if we don't see the person bleeding on the side of the road. And if we're narrow in our concerns—only worried about how practices and policies affect our own community or country—we'll miss God's heart for all nations and buy the lie that those "other" bloodied bodies aren't our concern. Remembering God's heart for all people and all nations helps us fight this tendency. As we consider the hardships being faced here and around the world, we begin to recognize how God might use us to aid in its healing.

## Remember the Author

God is the author of life. When he made man and woman in his image, he endowed them with inherent dignity. Our worth as humans isn't something we attain but something we *receive*. Likewise, God is the author of salvation. We never could have rescued ourselves by our own effort or merit, so he wrote the script of salvation: "By grace you have been saved through faith. And this is not your own doing; it is the gift of God, not a result of works, so that no one may boast" (Eph. 2:8–9). Though we may recognize him as the source of these great and glorious gifts, we tend to undermine his role in the day-to-day. But it is *God* who sovereignly knit us together in our mother's womb, determining our hair color and height and health. He's the source of our gifts and talents, the engineer of our boundaries and limitations. Our physical capacities, intellectual faculties, and contextual opportunities have been designed by him.

Remembering God's authorship keeps us from the kind of arrogance that ignores our neighbors out of self righteousness and judgment. It keeps us humble. What do we have that we did not receive?

Too often, we attribute our success to our own merit and feel entitled to a certain level of "blessing." We assume we deserve a particular lifestyle and view our various manifestations of covetousness, greed, and selfishness as perfectly reasonable. We might conclude that as long as we work hard, we have the right to use our resources in ways that primarily benefit us. But *everything* we have is from God and belongs to him. Anything we've accomplished or earned or built is ultimately due to him creating, sustaining, and empowering us. We're not, in fact, entitled to anything. It's all from him—which means that *all* we are and do should be used for his glory and our neighbors' good.

I could have been born in an impoverished agrarian society where my hard work consisted of growing just enough crops to survive each year. I could have been born in Somalia, where more than 10 percent of children die before their fifth birthday.[4] I could have been born to an alcoholic mother or an absent father and endured devastating trauma. I could have been born in a war-torn country and spent the majority of my life displaced. But I wasn't. God ordained for me to be born in a country and situation that provided me with countless advantages others lack. I did *nothing* to deserve this life. It's a gift from God.

It's easy to take whatever gifts we've received, whether it be our upbringing, natural talents, or education, for granted. We must remember that much of the success or prosperity we've enjoyed (and worked hard for) is objectively inaccessible to some, or accompanied by far greater hurdles to others. This will help us live with humble hearts and open hands as we care for neighbors in need. The more we appreciate God's provision for us, the more we'll want to steward our lives for the good of others.

God writes each of our stories. Some are marked by hardship and others by ease. But all of our stories—whether they are happy or tragic or somewhere in between—are meant to testify to the faithfulness of God, the author of redemption. Why is this so important to remember? Mercy never thrives among the proud. It's only when we embrace the fact that all we have is *from* Christ that we'll have the humility to offer it all for his service.

## Understanding Our Roles

There is only one hero in this story: the triune God. Apart from him, there is no hope. There is no redemption. But even though

4   Lucia Hug, David Sharrow, and Danzhen You, "Levels and Trends in Child Mortality: Report 2017," UNICEF (2017), https://www.unicef.org/.

he's the only hero, *our roles in his story still matter*. Usually tempted to either dismiss or exaggerate our roles, it's important to keep them in perspective. This affects not just how we look at ourselves, but how we see others—especially our neighbors in need. To be faithful doers of mercy, we must see ourselves and others in an accurate light.

*A Holistic View of Neighbors in Need*

There are multiple traps to avoid when we consider the poor and oppressed. One trap is to view them only as victims—victims of people or victims of tragic circumstances. Narrowly defining people in this way fails to regard their whole personhood. They are not just victims, but glorious image bearers of God. They have unique personalities and talents and may be incredibly resilient, creative, funny, or loyal. They may show great ingenuity amidst their poverty and bravery amidst their abuse.

People are more than their hardships. Though we should cultivate compassion and show love through action, we must never view people merely as spectacles for sympathy or projects we're trying to fix. To do so undermines their inherent dignity as human beings and alienates them from "the rest of us." It also makes our concern contingent on their state of suffering. When an orphan is adopted and ceases to be an orphan, do we no longer care? When a sexually trafficked woman is freed and rehabilitated, do we no longer care? To love as Jesus loves, we need to see the *whole person* and not just their pain.

It is also unhelpful to judge or romanticize those in need. We should never assume that people are suffering because of their own laziness or poor choices. Such a posture is arrogant and judgmental. We don't know what someone has gone through. We don't know what they've had to overcome. We don't know what injustices they've faced. Some of us are surrounded by environments far more conducive to human flourishing than others.

At the same time, being impoverished or oppressed *doesn't* make someone inherently virtuous either. Though we need soft and compassionate hearts, we should be wary of discounting the truth that all people are sinful and fraught with weakness. Otherwise we'll be left disillusioned and discouraged when we're inevitably awakened to the flaws of those we serve. This will ultimately limit our ability to be faithful extenders of mercy. Compassion simply will not endure if it's directed toward a fantasy.

Even when there's evidence that people are partially—or even *entirely*—responsible for their suffering, our call to mercy isn't extinguished. God has been so gracious to us, even when we've known better. It was the prodigal son's own fault that he found himself homeless and hungry, but that didn't stop the father from running to embrace him and throwing a feast to welcome him home (Luke 15:11–32).

Viewing the poor with level-headedness also grows our discernment about how to extend mercy. The more we understand the multifaceted reasons behind poverty, the more clarity we'll have to seek effective solutions. This helps direct our endeavors of mercy and enables us to identify ministries worthy of support.[5]

Worthwhile ministry models don't act as Band-Aids but seek to get to the root of problems through developed, long-term, and holistic approaches. There are times when short-term solutions are

---

5  The appendix includes questions for evaluating charitable organizations.

necessary. Some situations require a quick response—problems like natural disasters that leave so many lives wrecked, wars that displace people from their homes and countries, disease outbreaks. However, short-term solutions don't typically fix long-term problems (and often even exacerbate them). There is no cookie-cutter method to address poverty and injustice, and solutions that work well in one part of the world might not work in another. For these reasons, we must carefully implement and support endeavors of mercy that take the *whole* person into account.

As we faithfully tend to the physical needs of others, we must remember their preeminent need. The orphan, widow, poor, oppressed, sojourner, rejected, helpless, and weak are all sinners who don't need just the love of a great Father, but the forgiveness of a great Savior. More than they need relief from poverty or oppression, the suffering need Jesus.

*A Humble View of Ourselves*

Just as we need to cultivate a balanced view of the poor, we need to cultivate a balanced view of ourselves. In a Christian context, this requires humility regarding our role in the global mission. Too often we overemphasize what *we* have to offer. Our hearts may be filled with genuine love and a desire to serve the body, but if we don't recognize how limited our own perspectives are, we'll fail to discern how often we impose biblical principles through a distinctly Western lens.

God doesn't intend to reach the world through *Americans*, but to reach the world through his *disciples*. He is working through *all* his people—people of every race, nationality, ethnicity, ability, and socioeconomic status. We must fight our temptation toward saviorism, where we overemphasize our wisdom and power to "fix things." Nobody but Jesus has all the answers. And since he's at work in believers everywhere, we need the perspective of those who come from traditions and cultures different from ours. We *don't* always know better. In fact, it's essential to personal growth and collective sanctification to commit ourselves to learning from one another.

There's so much to learn from Christians who live in impoverished or persecuted nations. They're often compelling examples when it comes to fervent prayer and steadfastness through trial. They aren't under the same illusion of self-sufficiency that easily entangles the prosperous, and this leads to a deeper understanding of their reliance on God.

In other places, Christians live with a greater commitment to the local church. They don't have the luxury of "church shopping" or leaving a church amidst conflict to go to another one down the road, because there *isn't* another one down the road. So they learn to demonstrate the hard, biblical love that accompanies true commitment to a body of believers. They are compelled to walk through disagreement, conflict, and different preferences, in a way Christians here can avoid. (This isn't to imply it's always wrong to switch churches. But certainly the cavalier attitude in which leaving a church is often done—and how often it is attributable to an inability to work through conflict—is not a biblical one.)

Many times it's the poorest Christians who display the most extravagant generosity. They might have very little to give, but they give their meager offerings with great joy. I witnessed this in significant ways during my trips to India. I received lavish hospitality from Christians living in poor rural villages. I was given generous gifts of hair clips and markers from children who owned practically nothing. They cheerfully shared their very best, despite the uncomfortable fact that we were the rich and they were the poor. Oh, rather than being content to give our leftovers, let's follow the example of those who give their best amidst so little!

On the other hand, it's *false humility* to think that we (as in, Western Christians not suffering extreme persecution or poverty) have nothing to offer. We do! This is why the church consists of people all around the world. We are blessed with free access to Scripture and an abundance of resources that help us understand and apply it. This knowledge is a precious gift to share with Christians deprived of such resources and to new believers who are simply immature in their faith and understanding of what it means to follow Christ.

Sharing sound doctrine is a profound way to serve Christians living in parts of the world where Bibles are forbidden, Christians are scarce, and theology is mingled with tribal superstition. When we celebrate the strengths of believers in those contexts, it'd be foolish to dismiss the strengths we can offer them. As we diligently study God's word and develop doctrinal convictions, it's not for us to feel theologically superior but to be theologically generous.

Another resource we have to offer is our finances (we'll address this in greater depth later on). As a whole, American Christians are among the richest Christians in the world. We have a distinct opportunity to utilize our finances in ways that other Christians can't. We must never belittle the spiritual act of giving. Giving isn't a second-rate service; it's a profound expression of worship to God and act of love to others.

Imagine that there are ten people who desire to minister to marginalized, disabled women in Sri Lanka. Five of them live there and dedicate their time to building relationships and offering practical care. They arrange medical treatment and job assistance, and frequently provide meals. The other five people have "normal" careers and fund the ministry. They cover the expenses of the full-time ministry workers and finance the services being provided to the disabled women. Is one group more spiritual than the other? Absolutely not. Both are showing mercy, and both are necessary for the success of the ministry. The first group couldn't serve apart from the support of the second, and the second group would have nowhere to send their support apart from the service of the first group. This is why we can't allow our perceptions of mission to place those serving "on the ground" on a pedestal and diminish the value of other types of ministry. Putting mission into such a box disregards the diverse roles God calls and enables each of us to fill.

What a joy it is that God includes and equips us to alleviate the suffering of others for the glory of his name. What a privilege it is to not do it alone but to learn from and partner with believers all across the globe.

### Awaiting the Conclusion

Even though we're still in the in-between and not-yet-realized kingdom, we know what's coming. God has already revealed the conclusion of his great redemptive story. And to live in light of this conclusion, we need an eternal perspective. But what does that actually entail? I think this is a helpful summary: having an eternal perspective means we view our present world and its present troubles in light of the reality that Christ will return and usher in a kingdom that will last forever.

Here and now matters, but it's not all there is. Cultivating an eternal perspective helps us view the temporal through the lens of the eternal. It sees the here and now—and looks *past* the here and now.

When we actively await our eternal home, it dramatically transforms the way we live in this one. "If then you have been raised with Christ, seek the things that are above, where Christ is, seated at the right hand of God. Set your minds on things that are above, not on things that are on earth" (Col. 3:1–2). Remembering the magnificent fact that heaven is our true home and Christ our true King enables us to live fruitfully here. Setting our eyes on Christ as our prize diminishes the distractions that so often derail us. Our inclinations toward selfishness, apathy, and discontentment extinguish the more we behold the glory of God, and our fears begin to fade as we find confidence in his final victory.

Living in light of eternity inevitably loosens the grip of the world and rescues us from a wasted life. When we're not so distracted by meaningless pursuits—chasing the illusive idols of comfort, pleasure, success, and fame—we're free to dedicate our time and resources to the glory of God and good of our neighbors.

Living with an eternal perspective means we don't seek to find our belonging here. It helps us grow increasingly concerned that others accept the gift of the gospel and less concerned that they accept us. Fixing our eyes on eternity produces an urgency to spread the gospel because we remember the consequences awaiting those who remain separated from God. We grow a disdain for the fleeting joy of sin and anything that hinders our witness. We become less concerned with temporary pleasure, seeking instead Christ as our treasure. And the more we treasure him, the more we'll testify of his surpassing worth. We'll gladly pour out our lives and sacrifice for the good of others as we imitate Christ, who "for the joy that was set before him endured the cross" (Heb. 12:2).

A commitment to loving and serving our neighbors for the glory of God is difficult. It requires patience and commitment and endurance. Scripture encourages us:

> Let us not grow weary of doing good, for in due season we will reap, if we do not give up. So then, as we have opportunity, let us do good to everyone, and especially to those who are of the household of faith. (Gal. 6:9–10)

An eternal perspective lightens the burdens that weigh us down. As we look forward to the promise of eternal glory, God enables us to view our afflictions as light and momentary (2 Cor. 4:17). We'll be strengthened to fight the good fight—even when it's harder than we ever thought possible—compelled by the confidence that the war has already been won. We *can* have peace, our troubles *will* cease, because Christ defeated sin and death and reigns forevermore.

Our story has a good ending. But God isn't done yet. We're still in the chapter where he is saving and healing and redeeming and restoring. And rather than leaving us as useless side characters, he's chosen us to join in his good work.

**Discussion Questions**

1. Why is it important to view the brokenness of our present world in light of God's grand redemptive story? How does this guard us from both naïve optimism and hopeless pessimism?

2. In what areas of your life do you tend to take credit for your success or circumstances? How can you foster gratitude toward God and humility toward others?

3. In what situations are you tempted to judge the poor and needy? Why is it important to have a balanced, charitable, and holistic perspective to care for others well?

4. Read Colossians 3:1–2. Consider your day-to-day. In what ways are you setting your mind "on things that are above"? In what ways are you struggling not to be preoccupied with the "things that are on earth"?

2

# Who Is My Neighbor?

WITH THE GRAND NARRATIVE of redemption as our back-
drop, let's consider another story found in the Gospel of Luke
(10:25–37).

Once, a lawyer wanted to test Jesus. Feigning humility, he
asked, "Teacher, what shall I do to inherit eternal life?"

Jesus replied, "What is written in the Law? How do you
read it?"

Now, this lawyer was a good and upstanding Jewish man. He
paid attention in Hebrew school and knew the Torah inside and
out. Without missing a beat, he responded, "You shall love the
Lord your God with all your heart and with all your soul and
with all your strength and with all your mind, and your neighbor
as yourself."

It was a solid answer. Biblically faithful, theologically sound.
But it wasn't coming from a sincere heart. Unimpressed by the
lawyer's charade, Jesus responded, "You have answered correctly;
do this, and you will live."

Something about Jesus's answer bothered the lawyer—the term *neighbor* is ambiguous. So he, "desiring to justify himself," asked for clarification. "And who is my neighbor?"

In response, Jesus tells what is now a familiar parable:

> "A man was going down from Jerusalem to Jericho, and he fell among robbers, who stripped him and beat him and departed, leaving him half dead. Now by chance a priest was going down that road, and when he saw him he passed by on the other side. So likewise a Levite, when he came to the place and saw him, passed by on the other side. But a Samaritan, as he journeyed, came to where he was, and when he saw him, he had compassion. He went to him and bound up his wounds, pouring on oil and wine. Then he set him on his own animal and brought him to an inn and took care of him. And the next day he took out two denarii and gave them to the innkeeper, saying, 'Take care of him, and whatever more you spend, I will repay you when I come back.' Which of these three, do you think, proved to be a neighbor to the man who fell among the robbers?" He said, "The one who showed him mercy." And Jesus said to him, "You go, and do likewise." (Luke 10:30–37)

It's hard to admit, but we're susceptible to acting just like this lawyer. Wanting to avoid the discomfort of conviction, we can seek to justify ourselves for our lack of mercy. We're tempted to embrace a rigid understanding of "neighbor" and then add limitations and excuses in an effort to absolve ourselves when we neglect neighborly love. *I don't have time. It's not safe. I have my own family to worry about. I don't have a burden for that. I don't owe them anything. Someone else can do it. They got themselves into that mess. It's not like I can fix everything.* And on. And on. And on. We have mastered the art of making excuses.

Like the lawyer, we want to narrow what Jesus means by "neighbor." We assume it to mean our family and friends, maybe co-workers and residents on our street. We're also tempted to restrict how far we're willing to go to express neighborly love. It should be safe. Convenient. Responsible. *Not* extravagant.

But Jesus turns that kind of thinking on its head. Through a brief parable, he provides clear direction about being a good neighbor. He shows us how far *neighbor* is meant to extend and that true mercy involves risk, time, and generosity to care for those in need.

## A Different Kind of Neighbor

Jesus chose an unlikely setting for his story. The trek from Jerusalem to Jericho spanned 17 miles of treacherous terrain—not the kind of place people liked to go. He also chose unexpected characters. Given the hostility between Jews and Samaritans, the lawyer wouldn't have considered this a compelling example of obedience to the command to love your neighbor (especially since the despised Samaritan got to be the hero). But Jesus intentionally told a story that demonstrated how neighborly love stretches outside the boundaries we instinctively create. It includes people we don't know, people outside our communities, people of other ethnicities, and even those we might consider our enemies.

What does this mean for us today? In our modern age, we can show mercy in ways that were impossible at other points in history. There is exhaustive information available at our fingertips to learn how we can respond to problems like human trafficking, child marriage, and famine. When a natural disaster devastates a city halfway around the world, there's a good chance we can donate to provide aid. We can sponsor impoverished children to receive a better education, provide wheelchairs to those who don't have any, and stock refugee resettlement camps with supplies. The opportunities are endless.

But we are finite. We can't be aware of every need, support every worthy ministry, or even intercede for every people group. Frustrating as it is, we must embrace our God-given limitations. Otherwise the overwhelming poverty and suffering of the world will crush us with unwarranted guilt over our lack of power to fix it or paralyze us from doing anything at all. The limitations we experience aren't flaws to fight against; they're a part of our nature as created beings. They remind us that we are *not* God. So Jesus's parable shouldn't be understood as a charge to care for *every* neighbor, which is impossible. It's a charge to care for *any kind* of neighbor. Even as we accept our limitations, we can reflect the compassion Jesus commends: a compassion that is deep and wide and looks past common confines to alleviate the suffering of strangers.

## A Task Full of Risk

Jesus's parable also sets the stage for the risky task of loving our neighbors. It was dangerous for the Samaritan to even approach the bloodied body. The gruesome scene testified to the peril—what if an ambush awaited anyone who stopped to help? Surely this is one reason the Pharisee and the Levite passed by. It's easy to judge them, but how often do our actions reflect the same type of fear? How often does some sort of threat prevent us from seeking and serving the afflicted? Understanding these temptations, Jesus shows that compassion compels us to respond in mercy to the suffering, even at personal risk.

One of the greatest detriments to being the neighbors Christ has called us to be is fear. Sometimes, fear is what keeps us from sharing the good news of the gospel, though we know people who are under God's wrath and in need of his grace. Sometimes, fear of the unknown keeps us from pursuing adoption, though there are countless children in need of families. Sometimes, fear of financial insecurity keeps us from giving generously, though there are people sick, starving, and suffering because of abject poverty. Sometimes, fear of people's opinions keeps us from speaking against injustice, though our silence speaks volumes to the oppressed we ignore. Sometimes, fear of terrorism causes us to recoil from welcoming the refugee, though it relegates them to displacement, destruction, and despair. Sometimes, fear of discomfort keeps us from living with less and giving more, though the corruption of our consumerism often hurts the laborer we disregard.

And somehow, instead of identifying our fear as sinful we often call it by another name: *wisdom*.

Of course, wisdom itself isn't the problem here—the problem is when fear masquerades as wisdom. The book of Proverbs is full of instruction to seek wisdom, pursue counsel, avoid folly, plan ahead, and be faithful stewards. Christians are called to be thoughtful and discerning people.

The simple believes everything,
    but the prudent gives thought to his steps.

One who is wise is cautious and turns away from evil,
  but a fool is reckless and careless. (Prov. 14:15–16)

Jesus's parable isn't a call to recklessness, but to loving risk. It's not a rejection of wisdom, but an invitation to walk in true wisdom—the kind that fears the Lord. The more we walk in the fear of the Lord, the less other fears will factor into our decisions.

Trust in the LORD with all your heart,
  and do not lean on your own understanding.
In all your ways acknowledge him,
  and he will make straight your paths.
Be not wise in your own eyes;
  fear the LORD, and turn away from evil. (Prov. 3:5–7)

When I was in college, I suspended support for a child I'd been sponsoring. My reasoning: I was going broke paying for tuition and wanted to be *wise*. Before stopping the sponsorship I'd already cut most personal spending—I wouldn't go to the movies with friends or shop for new clothes and rarely ate out. So my decision to discontinue the sponsorship wasn't rooted in selfishness. However, I *feared* going into debt. God had generously provided me with a great job and affordable tuition rates, but rather than imitating his generosity, I clung to every penny. While it was wise to minimize spending on optional things for *myself*, godly wisdom compels generosity toward *others*, and fear prevented me from living generously throughout college.

Mistaking fear for wisdom will hinder us from showing mercy in all sorts of ways. It will keep us from serving in *those* neighborhoods, ministering to *those* people, and taking *those* risks. Sometimes, "being wise" is just a mask for being afraid.

The temptation to idolize physical safety is especially prevalent for parents. It wasn't until becoming a mom that I fully recognized how my parents had to overcome their own fears to let me serve in India for two months as a seventeen-year-old. Granted, there was every reason to believe it was a safe situation, but it's still unsettling to send your kid to the other side of the world. I'm grateful my parents trusted the Lord's leading rather than letting fear dictate the decision.

We can (and should) be thankful for whatever safety we enjoy, but we cannot let our appreciation *for* it become worship *of* it. I am so grateful the sound of warfare doesn't echo outside my house and that I don't experience PTSD like my refugee friends. I'm so grateful I can read my Bible in public, unlike so many of our persecuted brothers and sisters in Christ. I love going for walks in my well-lit and crime-free neighborhood at night. These are blessings to enjoy—glimpses of light in a dark world. But as a Christian, I also can't demand that God give me such circumstances. We live in a fallen world. If the Creator of the universe wasn't shielded from suffering when he walked the earth, should we expect a safe and easy road?

Jesus calls each of us to take up our cross to follow him, and taking up a cross is hazardous. We don't know the exact paths he will lead us down, but we can be sure of two things: living as faithful followers of Christ will include risk, but those risks can be engaged confidently because he will never leave or forsake us. He is present through every twist and turn and valley and obstacle and hardship and hurt. We can trust him, remembering the psalm of David: "Even though I walk through the valley of the shadow of death, I will fear no evil, for you are with me; your rod and your staff, they comfort me" (Ps. 23:4).

## Sacrificial Care

Jesus also illustrates in his parable that loving our neighbors involves sacrificial care. By using a strenuous journey as an example, Jesus implies that the Samaritan wasn't just meandering aimlessly but had an important reason for his travel. He had to sacrifice both time and plans in order to tend to the injured man. He carefully dressed his wounds. He hoisted the man onto his own animal and spent hours traveling to safety. Then not only did he stay all night to watch over him, but he promised to return.

Of all the implications of this parable, this one is the most challenging to me. Even as someone passionate about the priority of mercy-filled mission, I typically want it on *my* terms. I want to determine when and how it happens. I want to make the decision or commitment ahead of time. And while it's good to plan and prioritize, I can grow so consumed with day-to-day life that I'm prone to overlooking those around me. I resist embracing opportunities that are unexpected and inconvenient. But Jesus shows us that to be a good neighbor, we must sometimes allow our plans to be derailed.

The Samaritan also showed sacrificial love through his generosity. He paid the innkeeper two denarii to watch after the man— about the wage earned for two days of labor—and promised to cover any additional expenses incurred in his absence. Generosity like this isn't a planned part of someone's budget. The Samaritan didn't even know how much the final cost would be. But he loved the stranger as himself and sacrificed extravagantly out of concern for his well-being.

A lifestyle of generosity is primarily comprised of consistent and faithful acts of giving. But sometimes, as in this parable, God leads us down a road that exposes an *unexpected* need so that we can respond in unplanned generosity.

Several years ago, my husband and I encountered one of these unexpected opportunities. After learning about an antitrafficking organization working in Cambodia, we were gripped by the devastating need. The more we learned about the organization and its practices, the more intensely we wanted to support their efforts. There was one problem though: we were deep in the process of saving for adoption and had only a fraction of what we needed to fund it. Dipping into savings didn't seem like the right move when it was essential to prioritize adoption expenses. At the same time, the Holy Spirit's leading was too strong to ignore.

After wrestling through these conflicted feelings, I had an idea. Andrew's recent job change had him working from home four days a week (back before working remotely was common). This new dynamic meant that one of our two cars was left in the driveway most days. The solution was suddenly obvious: God had generously provided for our needs (and more), and selling our second car would enable us to give without affecting our adoption savings. After some prayer, Andrew enthusiastically agreed.

So we sold our second car, excitedly wrote a check to the ministry, and remained a one-car family for three years. Sure, it was inconvenient sometimes. But the cost of this choice was nothing compared to the joy we experienced in giving—and even the sense of "sacrifice" was a reflection of our own wealth. Maybe we didn't have expendable money in the bank, but most families don't own two cars either. Recognizing this helped stifle temptations we may have felt to swell in pride over a "radical" decision—if anything, selling our car for the purpose of giving only made us more aware of the abundance we already had.

## Good Neighbors Pay Attention

Finally, Jesus's story illustrates that good neighbors pay attention to the needs around them. If our hearts are preoccupied with our own circumstances, our minds fixated on our own schedules, and our eyes glued to our phones, we will miss opportunities to show mercy.

We must fight for awareness.

It's easy to forget particular expressions of poverty and oppression when they don't affect us. Theoretically, I know that children die of hunger-related causes every day. But in my comfy suburban neighborhood, that reality is difficult to remember. There aren't malnourished children sitting on the curb of my street who I can invite in for dinner. Need isn't always visible in my day-to-day life. So the only way for me to be responsive to many types of suffering is to intentionally look for it.

The problem is, it's natural to avoid thinking about the harsh realities of life in a broken world. Some situations are so devastating that we'd rather refrain from dwelling on them at all. On more than one occasion, I've been guilty of bemoaning, "That's horrific. I don't even want to think about it." But yielding to this inclination never drives us toward compassionate action.

What if that had been the attitude of Corrie and Betsie ten Boom, Dutch sisters who helped many Jews escape the Nazi Holocaust during World War II? The realities of the Holocaust are so hauntingly barbaric that some try to deny it happened at all. We don't want to believe that such large swathes of people could act with such measured ruthlessness. I imagine Corrie and Betsie were tempted to keep their heads down—to just generically lament the terrors of war. Instead, they opened their eyes to an entire people group that was being hunted down, dragged to prison camps, and slaughtered. Instead of clinging to a measure of naïvety about the evil happening, they risked their lives to aid over eight hundred Jewish men, women, and children.[1]

Of course, Corrie and Betsie ten Boom are a uniquely powerful example. And the whole point of this book is for ordinary people to see how God has equipped them for mercy. So moving on from these historical heroes, let me tell you about some people I know.

I think of all the foster parents in my church who willingly enter into heartache and court dates and unknowns and trauma so that they can provide loving care to hurting children. I think of my husband, who has navigated language barriers to build a friendship with a man who fled Syria after being kidnapped and tortured. I think of my friend Brenda, who has committed to love women trapped in addiction, even when that includes the agony of watching relapse after relapse.

People like Brenda aren't effective because they insulate themselves from harrowing realities, but, rather, in devotion to a faithful and sustaining God, they confront them and move toward heart-wrenching needs.

1  "The History of the Museum," Corrie ten Boom House, accessed January 9, 2023, https://www.corrietenboom.com/.

It's painful to acknowledge the troubles faced by many around the world: people on the brink of starvation, parents unable to provide medical intervention for their children, women abused by theirs husbands and oppressed by their governments, girls raped and sold as slaves, families left destitute in war-torn places, unborn babies torn apart in the womb meant to protect them, children abandoned or neglected by their parents, Christians persecuted for their faith. It's heartbreaking to dwell on any of these things, yet they can't be ignored.

Whenever one of us says, "I just can't handle thinking about it," compassion compels us to consider, *They can't handle living like that. God, how can I alleviate their burden?*

The church must be dedicated to hearing and attending to the cry of the afflicted. May all Christians, particularly those living in relative comfort (like me and probably you), resist the temptation to burrow our heads in the sand because we dread emotional upheaval.

Proverbs 21:13 soberly warns, "Whoever closes his ear to the cry of the poor will himself call out and not be answered." God takes our concern for the poor—or lack of it—very seriously. He is *not* apathetic to our apathy. Rather than closing our ears, hiding our eyes, and resting in ignorance, we are called to regularly and intentionally consider those who suffer so that we can regularly and intentionally respond to their cry.

Psalm 41:1 says, "Blessed is the one who considers the poor!" To *consider* implies thoughtful effort. Apart from careful consideration, we won't engage the dynamics of poverty and oppression in a meaningful way. We might even make problems worse; many a well-meaning person has. But if we diligently learn about the causes of and solutions to needs around us—and humbly seek biblical wisdom for how to engage them—the ignorance and false assumptions that prevent us from responding will begin to break down. Over time, the Lord will inevitably place burdens for *specific* needs, places, and people on our hearts. As he does this, our mercy will be most effective if we take the time to consider the multifaceted aspects of need, relevant background history, and approaches that have proven fruitful or vain. This helps us discern how to pray, what types of organizations to support, and how to practically serve.

Remember the car we sold? That story was the result of learning from those far wiser and more experienced than I. Our church was hosting a benefit concert to combat human trafficking. Without a particular charity in mind, I spent a lot of time researching and comparing organizations in order to identify the one to which our church would delegate funds. During this process, I found a compelling ministry working in Cambodia.

Prior to this, I knew *nothing* about Cambodia. I couldn't even place it on a map (geography was never my strong suit). I had absolutely no reason to care about this country—*until* I was compelled to learn about it.

Bear with me for an abbreviated history lesson.

I learned how intensely Cambodia suffered because of its proximity to the Vietnam War. The devastation inflicted by both Vietnam and the United States left the neutral country reeling and desperate for help. This paved the way for the Khmer Rouge to take its place as their savior before performing even worse terror. Eager to purify the country of all things associated with the West, the radical communist Khmer Rouge executed every person of education: teachers, business owners, doctors, nurses. This genocide killed *half* of the population, eradicated Cambodia's infrastructure, and left the entire country as a functional prison camp.

Fast-forward through a Vietnamese invasion, a civil war, and an embargo prohibiting international aid.

What happens? How does a country left with radical communists and children of the Killing Fields recover from complete devastation? How can a society begin to flourish when businesses have been annihilated, parents and professionals have been murdered, children are uneducated and indoctrinated, and all that remains is the residue of destruction?

A society built on such brutality will inevitably devalue life. At alarming rates, women and children were sexually trafficked. Until recent years, young children were a *common* commodity, openly sold to local and pedophile sex tourists. Little girls and boys were used and abused up to twenty times a day, every day. They endured unspeakable evil with no one to defend them and no law to prosecute their abusers.

As gut-wrenching as it was to learn about the affliction and corruption of Cambodia, my heart was lifted as I also learned how God was working. When at one time corrupt police officers owned half the brothels (many of which sold children), now there is an antitrafficking force dedicated to prosecuting such pimps. When at one time nobody would have spoken up for victims of sex trafficking because their experience was considered their Karma, the communal mindset has shifted to condemn such evil. When at one time there was no help to be found, now there are thriving ministries working to bring holistic healing.

Most importantly, I learned how the gospel is going forth. A racist murderer became a pastor to the very people group he formerly detested. Survivors of horrific abuse have experienced the healing love of Christ. Christ is forgiving, redeeming, and transforming these people.

Now you know a little more about Cambodia too. It is only one small part of the globe. And human trafficking is only one of many problems. But God cares about these specific people and problems. As his people, we should too.

God will lead us to different people in different corners of the world for different purposes. But may we all be eager to learn. May we all resonate with the powerful words of eighteenth-century abolitionist William Wilberforce: "You may choose to look the other way, but you can never say again that you did not know."[2]

Don't look the other way. In a world aching from adversities that are complicated to address, there are always more ways to learn and grow as doers of mercy.

## Learn from Other Good Neighbors

We all have heroes. As kids, these heroes wear capes or wield light sabers or dunk basketballs. As adults, our heroes mature into historical figures, revolutionaries, or experts in our fields of work. And as we tend to imitate those we admire, we should consider what qualities we're inclined to seek in our heroes.

2   William Wilberforce, close of speech in House of Commons (1791), cited in, Randy Alcorn, "You May Choose to Look the Other Way, But . . . ," Eternal Perspectives Ministries, https://www.epm.org/.

Are we more inspired by success or service? By wealth or generosity? By talent or faithfulness? It's certainly not wrong to admire things like athleticism, business prowess, or creative expression. God blesses the world with so many things to enjoy and to accomplish with excellence. But we should be *most* inspired by those who bear the fruit of the Spirit as they live as ambassadors of God's kingdom—even if they're just ordinary people faithfully serving in ordinary ways.

There are so many men and women throughout history who dedicated themselves to the ministry of mercy, who exemplified the kind of neighborly love expressed in Jesus's parable. There are "big names" with big stories, and unknown names with humble stories. We can learn from Amy Carmichael and Pandita Ramabai, who served exploited and destitute girls in India. We can learn from Frederick Douglass, who secretly taught fellow slaves to read Scripture, courageously helped others escape slavery, and prophetically challenged a "Christian" nation to repent for hating, enslaving, and tyrannizing Black men, women, and children. We can learn from George Müller, who cared for more orphans than he could afford, but for whom God always miraculously provided. We can learn from Hannah More, a poet and abolitionist of the eighteenth century, who used her gift of writing to influence powerful leaders in society.

And because the church is primarily comprised of people who will not etch into history and stories that seem insignificant, we can find heroes in the ordinary men, women, and children who live mercifully in everyday faithfulness: the teenager who uses her babysitting money to sponsor an impoverished child, the businessman who always mows the lawn for his widowed neighbor, the retired couple who shows hospitality to the homeless, the underprivileged family who still finds ways to share.

There are countless people to learn from—countless examples of weak people used in mighty ways who offered their meager loaves and fish to a God who multiplies.

Ultimately we learn to be loving neighbors by looking to Jesus. He is the good shepherd who looks after his sheep. He is the Servant-King who knelt and washed feet. He is the healer whose touch cured lepers and cast out demons. He is the rescuer who came from heaven to save us when we were as helpless and hopeless as the man beaten on the side of the road. The good Samaritan ultimately points to Jesus, who endured the greatest cost and paid the greatest price to save us. If we want to be good neighbors, we have only to look to him.

When we are overwhelmed by the brokenness of the world and frustrated over our lack of power to fix it, we must remember that the weight of the world is not on our shoulders but is in subjection under Christ's feet. There is only one Savior, whom we are not called to *be* but to *obey*. Remembering this keeps us from striving for the impossible—we don't seek to save our suffering neighbors but to love them as Christ instructed, as doers of mercy.

### Discussion Questions

1. Reread the parable of the good Samaritan (Luke 10:25–37). What most often tempts you to ignore the suffering of others? How would you like to grow?

2. Consider a time you took a risk or made a sacrifice to care for someone in need. How was God faithful to you through that?

3. What are practical ways God might be calling you to show mercy to someone? How do you plan to take action? What fears or desires might get in the way?

4. Which people or issues (e.g., trafficking, famine, homelessness) most stir your heart? How can you lean in and seek to learn more?

5. Who in your local church inspires you to be a good neighbor? Share about their examples.

3

# Imitators of God

I INHERITED MY DAD'S NOSE. It's got a big bump on it just like his, and his mother's, and—I'm not sure how many generations this trait goes back. We see these little resemblances all the time. *She's got her dad's eyes. He's got his mom's smile.* But it's not just physical resemblances we notice. My daughter is adopted from India. She has beautiful brown skin, deep chocolate eyes, and curly black hair. She doesn't look anything like us in appearance. But if you spend enough time with her, you'd find that she's picked up various quirks and qualities of being our daughter. She's definitely a DiMarcangelo.

We're all reflections, in some way, of those around us. We talk like them or dress like them or think like them or act like them. For better or worse, we can't help but be shaped by others.

But there is one shaping influence that matters most, one family resemblance we *must* share: as beloved children of God, we are called to be imitators of him (Eph. 5:1). From the moment we are adopted into God's family, we are called to look more and more like our Father. And because we've been united to the Son and filled with the Spirit, we *will* look more and more like him.

There are, of course, many ways to grow as imitators of God. But for the purpose of this book, we are going to look at our calling to reflect his heart of compassion and justice as we devote ourselves to the good work of mercy.

## Reflecting Our Father's Compassion

God has created us to follow him with our *entire* being. We're not simply called to obey in action; we're called to share his heart. The more we're transformed into his likeness, the more our emotions mirror his. We begin to *feel* what he feels.

And our God is a God of compassion.

But what exactly does *compassion* mean? Compassion is a "sympathetic consciousness of others' distress together with a desire to alleviate it,"[1] and "a feeling of deep sympathy and sorrow for another who is stricken by misfortune, accompanied by a strong desire to alleviate that suffering."[2] Consider those phrases: "sympathetic consciousness," "strong desire to alleviate," "deep sympathy and sorrow." Compassion is something we feel in the depths of our heart. By its very definition, compassion evokes strong emotion. Compassionate people aren't emotionally detached. They're not just going through the motions and trying to do the right thing. Those filled with compassion deeply value others, grieve with them in their sorrow, and have a restless

1   *Merriam-Webster*, s.v. "compassion," accessed January 6, 2023, https://www.merriam -webster.com/.
2   Dictionary.com, s.v. "compassion," accessed January 6, 2023, https://www.dictionary .com/.

desire to ease their suffering. And isn't that the heart of God? He moves toward us in our suffering, shares in our pain, and offers us comfort.

Ever since sin ushered suffering into the world, God has demonstrated his heart for the hurting. When his people were enslaved, oppressed, and exiled, he had compassion and heard their cries. Even when their suffering was the self-inflicted consequence of their own sin, he had compassion for them.

> Some sat in darkness and in the shadow of death,
>     prisoners in affliction and in irons,
> for they had rebelled against the words of God,
>     and spurned the counsel of the Most High. . . .
> Some were fools through their sinful ways,
>     and because of their iniquities suffered affliction. . . .
> Then they cried to the LORD in their trouble,
>     and he delivered them from their distress.
>         (Ps.107:10–11, 17, 19)

What amazing love!

His heart of compassion is also revealed through Old Testament law. The Israelites were set apart to live differently from the pagan nations surrounding them—to reflect what God and his kingdom were like. So he wrote into his law provisions for the fatherless, the widow, the poor, and even those outside the house of Israel—the sojourners (Lev. 23:22; 25:35–43; Deut. 24:17–22). He cared so deeply about their provision and protection that he gravely warned any who would mistreat and ignore them (Exod. 22:21–27; 23:6–8; Ezek. 16:49–50).

In the New Testament many accounts testify to the compassion of Jesus. "Jesus went throughout all the cities and villages, teaching in their synagogues and proclaiming the gospel of the kingdom and healing every disease and every affliction. When he saw the crowds, he had compassion for them, because they were harassed and helpless, like sheep without a shepherd" (Matt. 9:35–36). When he saw a widow grieving over the death of her son, he had compassion on her and raised him back to life (Luke 7:11–17).

Jesus proclaimed the gospel and healed the sick for the glory of his name *and* because he had deep compassion for the people. He saw the sorry state of their souls and their circumstances and was so moved by compassion that he reached out to comfort them in their sorrows, heal their afflictions, and offer them the hope of the coming kingdom. Even when the timing was terrible—such as after the execution of his cousin John the Baptist—Jesus had compassion on the crowds seeking him and interrupted his own grief to heal their sick (Matt. 14:14).

Later Jesus noticed the hunger pangs of the crowd around him and told his disciples, "I have compassion on the crowd because they have been with me now three days and have nothing to eat. And I am unwilling to send them away hungry, lest they faint on the way" (Matt. 15:32). I love that. Jesus was *unwilling* to send them away hungry. Their discomfort was only temporary, but he was too concerned to let them faint in hunger. Of course, so much more was at stake. The miracles Jesus performed always pointed to his identity as King of the universe. But they also pointed to his heart. Jesus shows us that we don't just serve a powerful God who can do miracles; we serve a compassionate God who *notices* and *cares* about the needs of his creatures. He is not aloof to our discomfort.

Story after story reveals our Lord's compassion. He is tender toward the physically afflicted—those enduring disability and disease. His heart aches for the impoverished and the mistreated. His concern stretches to the orphan, the widow, the sojourner, the outcast, and the grieving. He has such compassion for the lost that he endured the humility of the cross and the judgment of God. It was his compassion that created a way of redemption for sinners to be forgiven and loved as his children. Apart from his great compassion, we'd have no redeemer to rescue us from holy wrath.

When we grow in understanding the depth of God's compassion for us, the hindrances that prevent us from imitating his compassion will begin to crumble. Rather than being emotionally detached from the suffering of others—or simply going through the motions of good works—we'll be filled with a loving and earnest desire to ease their suffering. We'll learn to grieve with those who grieve. We'll pour ourselves out for the sake of others. Compassion for lost souls will stir us to share the gospel, despite opposition. Compassion for the poor will make generosity a joy instead of a burden, because we're so eager to alleviate their suffering. Without compassion *for* others, our motivation to express mercy *to* others often lies in guilt and obligation, making our obedience wearisome. Compassion ignites our zeal and strengthens our resolve to obey.

Compassion isn't just for "bleeding hearts"; it's a trait that should mark every disciple of Jesus. And if we lack compassion for those experiencing pain, poverty, or oppression, we must repent and ask the Spirit to help us change. Scripture instructs, "*Put on* then, as God's chosen ones, holy and beloved, compassionate hearts" (Col. 3:12). We have an active role in this. True compassion always compels action. We cannot be content to be oblivious, apathetic, or callous toward suffering. In Christ, our hearts are made new—enabled to beat with compassion as we bend to serve our neighbors.

### Reflecting Our Father's Love of Justice

Justice is a core component of the gospel. We were enemies of God, objects of his holy wrath because of our wicked rebellion. But even while God was angry, he had compassion on us and orchestrated a way to satisfy justice *and* provide salvation. He sent his Son as the atoning sacrifice for our sins. Jesus absorbed every ounce of wrath we deserved. Without God's righteous fury toward sin, sinners wouldn't need a Savior. The cross would've been pointless. God's anger and justice are intrinsically tied to the good news of the gospel, assuring us that someday he will make all things right.

Injustice is a symptom of living in a fallen world. God made all people in his image, and yet over the millennia sin has maintained the oppression of others based on their ethnicity, nationality, religion, sex, appearance, cognitive and physical abilities, and social status. The sickness of sin runs deep in all humanity's veins—some of us just have more opportunity to act upon it. So the powerful target the weak, the greedy prey on the poor, the proud show partiality, and whole people groups are marginalized and mistreated.

This grieves God. His rage burns toward those who ignore his commands and enact injustice. His ear is attuned to the cry of the oppressed, and he even promises vengeance on their behalf. Exodus vividly portrays this holy wrath:

You shall not wrong a sojourner or oppress him, for you were sojourners in the land of Egypt. You shall not mistreat any widow or fatherless child. If you do mistreat them, and they cry out to me, I will surely hear their cry, and my wrath will burn, and I will kill you with the sword, and your wives shall become widows and your children fatherless. (Exod. 22:21–24)

If our Holy God so hates injustice, how are we, as sinful beings, to engage oppression? While it might seem surprising to state this in a book about mercy, one essential reaction is *anger*.

Yep, you read that right.

Righteous anger is a way we reflect God's character. He cares for those who are mistreated *because he loves them*. Likewise, when we feel anger about the oppression of others it demonstrates love for them. When children are molested and women abused, we should be angry. When terrorism and violence destroy families, communities, and countries, we should be angry. When wicked governance enables abortion and racism to thrive, we should be angry. And when perpetrators of evil aren't held accountable, we should be angry. I would argue that if injustice doesn't make us angry, it reveals that our hearts lack love, and we haven't understood something about God.

The oppression of others *must* move us, because if we truly value people as image bearers of God—regardless of their age, ability, ethnicity, religion, or status—we'll experience visceral reactions when they're mistreated. That said, while anger should be a righteous display of love for God and others, it's often tainted by our own sin and self-righteousness. We must continually seek the Spirit's help, asking him to humble us and sanctify our anger. It's only the supernatural work of the Spirit that enables us to desire both justice and salvation for those affected by evil *and* the perpetrators of it. Just as our Savior interceded on behalf of those who mocked, mistreated, and crucified him—just as he interceded for *us*—the Spirit can help us intercede for those deserving condemnation.

I'll be honest though: sometimes this feels impossible. Who wants to pray for someone who's molested a child or raped a woman or murdered an innocent man? I sure don't, and I think I'm in good company. But as sinners made saints, we are called to walk the difficult line of maintaining a righteous anger against injustice and a tender-hearted desire for God to save those who inflict it.

God sees the ugliness of sin far more clearly than we do, but he still sent his Son to die for the sins of the world. He made a way for justice and mercy to coexist, for judgment and grace to harmonize. Just as Christ paid for *my* sin and wickedness when he died on the cross for me, his blood is enough to cover every form of evil expressed by man.

Furthermore, we can trust that God will *not* allow evil to go unpunished. Our justice systems may be flawed, but his isn't. He is the perfect judge. No bribe can sway him. No evidence escapes his notice. No evil goes unchecked. So when we're troubled by injustice, especially when it seems like people are getting away with it, we can take heart. There will be justice—either at the cross or before the final judgment seat.

Holding fast to the hope of God's perfect justice also protects us from living in a *perpetual* state of anger. If we don't understand the purpose and limitations of anger, it will burn us out. Since evil is always present in the world, there is always something we could be angry about, but living in perpetual anger only leads to cynicism and despair. As Christians, we can experience anger and still be marked by hope and peace because we're confident God's justice will prevail.

Further, righteous anger toward injustice isn't meant to be a solely emotional experience; it's meant to *lead* us somewhere—into the pursuit of justice. Anger is the jumpstart to action. It's like the match, but love and faith and hope are the fuel. When Jesus taught us to pray, "Your kingdom come, your will be done, on earth as it is in heaven" (Matt. 6:10), he was reminding us that we're not supposed to passively wait for his kingdom—we're called to seek it. Here. Now. The church is meant to show the world what the kingdom of heaven is like, so we pursue righteousness, justice, and peace as we expectantly await our King's return.

The founder of the antitrafficking organization I've referred to in this book has a background as a forensic scientist for the Canadian police force. Using his expertise, he helped secure the convictions of men guilty of sexual assault and worked with Cambodian law enforcement to extend shoddy sentencing for these heinous crimes. However, his organization *also* partners with another ministry dedicated to proclaiming the gospel to those same convicts. What a compelling example of executing earthly justice and extending undeserved grace, of pursuing the kingdom now, while also pointing to the kingdom to come!

As we seek to share God's heart, we must faithfully engage all kinds of injustices, both popular and unpopular. It is good and right to fight against human trafficking. Such work (usually) attracts support regardless of political affiliations or religious backgrounds. It is also good and right to confront the injustice of abortion and racism. But depending on the context you're in, speaking to those issues will garner either applause or accusation. This is why *God's word* must inform how we engage justice issues, rather than our politics or experiences or the cultural norms around us. As we study Scripture and humbly learn from others, God will grow our discernment and help us actively "learn to do good; seek justice, correct oppression; bring justice to the fatherless, [and] plead the widow's cause" (Isa. 1:17).

## But I Don't Want to Get Political

Given the amount of political landmines that exist today, we're often tempted to avoid issues of injustice, hiding behind the excuse of not "wanting to get political." But it doesn't matter whether something is perceived as a conservative or liberal agenda. As citizens of heaven, our allegiance is to God. We're called to reflect the ethics of *his* kingdom, whether others agree with us or not. Sometimes this allegiance even means disobeying man-made laws in order to honor God's law. Isaiah declares,

> Woe to those who decree iniquitous decrees,
>     and the writers who keep writing oppression,
> to turn aside the needy from justice
>     and to rob the poor of my people of their right,
> that widows may be their spoil,
>     and that they may make the fatherless their prey!
>         (Isa. 10:1–2)

When laws are corrupt, enabling the powerful to prey on the weak and mistreat the poor, Christians are called to action. Devotion to God led the Hebrew midwives to disobey Pharaoh's orders to kill male Hebrew children (Exod. 1:15–20). Devotion to God led Harriet Tubman to help slaves escape to freedom. Devotion to God led Corrie ten Boom to hide Jews from the Nazis. Devotion to God led John Perkins—and countless others during the civil rights movement—to confront the evil laws of segregation. Sometimes submission to God entails resisting and rebelling against human authority.

A final thought, but I think it's an important one. It's often assumed that as long as we aren't personally involved in perpetuating injustice, there's no reason to get involved. We wash our hands and declare, "It's not my problem." However, Isaiah combats this mindset with the call to correct oppression. Now, we don't live in a theocracy as the Israelites did. I'm not saying that we should fight for power so we can force people to live out biblical ethics. But please hear this: not being a part of the problem doesn't negate our responsibility to be a part of the solution. As the church—an embodied picture of God's kingdom—we must consider how to steward our influence and opportunities to correct the oppressive effects of sin.

In whatever settings we have a voice, and toward whatever situations we're aware, we should be pursuers of justice. Whether in regard to children suffering abuse, women being trafficked, immigrants being taken advantage of, minorities experiencing racial prejudice, the disabled being devalued, or the innocent being executed, the opportunities to seek justice abound. When Christians expend effort to correct injustices, we testify to the dignity of life and point to the goodness and perfect justice of God.

### Dedicated to Good Works of Mercy

As our hearts are increasingly inclined toward compassion, and we grow a yearning for justice, the inevitable response is a life dedicated to good works.

Since salvation is by grace alone, emphasizing works feels, well, dangerous. We're tempted to equate it to legalism and worry about compromising the doctrine of grace. But the Bible speaks frequently about good works. Why? Because our lives are meant to shine like a spotlight on the God at work within us. We don't do good works so we would be seen, but so that *he* would be. "You are the light of the world. . . . Let your light shine before others, *so that* they may see your good works and give glory to your Father who is in heaven" (Matt. 5:14, 16).

Good works point others to behold our good God.

The book of James has made many a grace-saturated Christian uncomfortable with its frank treatment of works in relation to faith. For instance, James writes:

> What good is it, my brothers, if someone says he has faith but does not have works? Can that faith save him? If a brother or sister is poorly clothed and lacking in daily food, and one of you says to them, "Go in peace, be warmed and filled," without giving them the things needed for the body, what good is that? So also faith by itself, if it does not have works, is dead. (James 2:14–17)

Good works certainly encompass more than offering provision to the poor. But the fact that James utilizes this specific example is reflective of two things: *God's* compassion for the poor as he charges believers to care for them, and the sinful tendency to neglect this work and *feign* care through empty prayers. These verses are "an illustration of what faith without works looks like in everyday life. In itself the phrase 'Go in peace, be warmed and filled' is a pious wish and prayer for the welfare of the poor, but in reality it is a cop-out, masking a refusal to help the person in need."[3] Prayer is absolutely crucial—but it's not a substitute for mercy-filled works.

This should sober us. James declares that faith is *dead* if it's not accompanied by works. When such works are absent, Scripture points us to seriously question the genuineness of our faith. Why? Because belief can't stand alone. After all, "Even the demons believe—and shudder!" (James 2:19). The demons know God is one. They know he is King of the universe. They know he is sovereign and eternal and righteous and holy. They *believe*, but they don't submit. James's words are a warning. It's so much easier—so much more comfortable—to believe the right things without being changed by them. Yet orthodoxy (right belief) must not be separated from orthopraxy (right conduct). A dedication to good works of mercy and justice is not an optional side gig for the Christian but the *inevitable* fruit of being God's children. Saving faith always produces good works.

It's also crucial to address spiritual *and* physical needs, not embracing one at the neglect of the other. The gospel is the most precious gift we can share, but how will people believe we care about their souls if we don't care about their bodies? How will

---

3   *ESV Study Bible*, ed. Wayne Grudem (Wheaton, IL: Crossway, 2008), note on James 2:15–16.

we convince them of our concern for their eternal state if we lack concern for their temporal one? It's not that acts of mercy are more important than sharing the gospel, but they do legitimize our witness. We shouldn't fool ourselves into thinking it's possible to ignore the physical needs of others (if God has given us means and opportunity to meet those needs) and still be living as faithful disciples of Jesus. The two are irreconcilable. Good works of mercy bear witness to our faith.

God charges the rich—which includes many of us when considering global and historical standards—to be rich in good works:

> As for the rich in this present age, charge them not to be haughty, nor to set their hopes on the uncertainty of riches, but on God, who richly provides us with everything to enjoy. They are to do good, to be rich in good works, to be generous and ready to share, thus storing up treasure for themselves as a good foundation for the future, so that they may take hold of that which is truly life. (1 Tim. 6:17–19)

Being rich in good works means that our lives are marked with an abundance, extravagance, and overflow of them. They aren't few and far between. It doesn't mean volunteering at a homeless shelter once a year or sporadically giving to charity when the inspiration hits. Being rich in good works means that they are lavish and plentiful throughout our whole lives. It could be regularly visiting a nursing home, making meals for a chronically sick neighbor, aiding a child with special needs in Sunday school, or tutoring underprivileged students. It could be routinely dropping off diapers for a parent in need or driving resettled refugees to their appointments. Whatever form our service takes, it's a recurrent—not rare—priority in our lives.

God isn't just interested in refining our actions though; he's intent on renewing our hearts. Jesus gave himself to redeem us from lawlessness and to purify for himself a people *zealous* for good works (Titus 2:14). They're not just something we do but something we enthusiastically and eagerly pursue. They aren't a chore but a privilege, not a burden but a joy. As the Holy Spirit fills us with zeal, we grow determined to continue in good works despite the cost.

And as our *devotion* to good works grows (Titus 3:8), we'll be intentional to carry them out regardless of inconvenience. We'll remain committed to press on, even when it's monotonous and mundane or harder than we ever anticipated. There are so many people who display this type of devotion. I could fill this entire book with their stories and examples. But I'm going to tell you just one.

Jayme had four kids, worked part-time as a nurse, and home-schooled her children when a church friend asked if she'd be willing to help a struggling family. There were two young girls left in the care of their great-grandmother after their mother went to prison, and between the great-grandmother's age, illness, and poverty, she needed support. Lots of it. Jayme agreed to help with childcare and babysat frequently for well over a year. She never asked or expected to get paid and managed all the transportation. Whenever the great-grandmother was sick, she'd welcome the girls into her home for days—sometimes weeks—at a time. Given her full schedule and the unpredictability and demands of childcare, most people wouldn't have blamed her if she pulled back. Instead, she was so committed that she eventually opened her home when the girls needed a place to live long-term. It didn't end there either. Along with caring for the girls, she built relationships with the entire family. She called and visited the great-grandmother until her death and sought to befriend and support the girls' mom when she was released from prison. And after many twists and turns—too many to share here—she eventually welcomed a *different* member of that extended family as her son. When Jayme first agreed to help with babysitting, she never anticipated the roller-coaster ahead of her. It was filled with love, grief, confusion, heartbreak, joy, and countless tears. This type of costly love—and the profound fruit it bears—just doesn't happen apart from deep devotion.

We aren't saved by good works, but we are redeemed *for* good works (Eph. 2:10). God didn't redeem for himself a people to live for themselves, but a people to live for him. As redeemed children, our lives should be marked by zealous devotion to good works for the glory of our Father.

## Gratitude Is the Fuel of Mercy

Ultimately, it is because we have been *recipients* of the greatest mercy that we extend mercy to others. The most perfect expression of compassion and justice was accomplished by our triune God. He had compassion on our helpless, hopeless, and hell-bound state. We were both unwilling and unable to rescue ourselves, so he initiated the alleviation of our suffering. He satisfied the just penalty for sin, bringing hope to all sinners, and executed perfect justice, bringing comfort to all who are oppressed. It was *his* good work that sealed our redemption.

Gratitude for the mercy we've received is the fuel that ignites our mercy toward others. Few qualities diminish our witness faster than living as ungrateful Christians. Being overly preoccupied with our own problems distracts us from serving others, and expressing bitterness over our circumstances prevents others from beholding the beauty of Christ through our lives. Gratitude makes us look *up*, which enables us to look *out*. Ingratitude buries us in a void of unhappiness where there's room for nobody but ourselves. It makes us bitter and only aware of what we lack instead of what we have. Gratitude energizes us to serve those who suffer (even if we're struggling ourselves) and enhances our witness to the unbelieving world as they see the paradox of a life marked by gratitude amidst grief.

The people most dedicated to good works of mercy and justice usually aren't those who have the easiest lives, but those who are the most grateful for the lives they have. This isn't the artificial fruit of positive self-talk or an avoidance of facing sorrow or toxic positivity. It is because their deep lament has driven them to drink of the fountain of living waters—and they have tasted and seen that God is good.

Maira has been a committed member of my church for over twenty years. She is a meek and gentle woman who is fiercely passionate about the gospel mission. For as long as I've known her, she's someone who beams with gratitude and pours out her life in service to others. She has deep compassion toward the suffering and a humble desire to grow in mercy. What makes Maira's example so powerful, though, is that she's walked through quite a bit of suffering herself.

Her daughter was only three when she was diagnosed as legally blind. For a period, Maira grieved over what this might mean for her daughter's future. Would she ever read? Would she ride a bike? Would her blindness steal her happy disposition? God comforted Maira in her grief and enabled her to find joy in the new normal. With each new challenge and temptation to be fearful, God proved himself faithful.

Years later, and shortly after her husband, Ken, started serving in pastoral ministry at our church, he got sick. His health deteriorated so rapidly that he had to step down from ministry and go on disability. Eventually, he was diagnosed with a rare and excruciatingly painful disease. He lost an alarming amount of weight and experienced such agonizing pain that he couldn't even bear to be touched. His disease gave Maira heart-wrenching questions to consider, like how to prepare for widowhood.

By God's grace, Ken finally went into remission five years later. Maira recalls those painful days with acute clarity—severe suffering isn't easily forgotten. But Maira also remembers how God sustained her. "This is God's story of faithfulness," she told me, "all my trials flowed through the sieve of his love for me."

Even amidst the constraints of her trying and changing circumstances, Maira has always been eager to participate in God's mercy-filled mission. She has never put it off, waiting for a more convenient time. During seasons that kept her homebound, she wrote letters of encouragement to persecuted Christians. When she was the primary caretaker for her aging father, she brought him along to church outreach events even though it took more time and effort to include him. When her schedule was busy taking her dad to doctor's visits, she learned to crochet and spent her time in waiting rooms making scarves for teens aging out of the foster system.

Today she organizes charitable-collection events at the library where she works, brings tracts and Bibles to give away on vacation, and keeps snacks on hand to share with homeless people. She sponsors orphaned children and regularly writes them letters and prays for their home countries. She is always reading and learning about mercy ministries and shares what she learns with others.

Over the years, in small ways and big, Maira has borne a striking resemblance to her heavenly Father. Rather than growing resentful over the hardships she's endured, she's lived in wonder of God's goodness to her and sought to relieve the suffering of others.

I want to be that kind of person.

If we want to grow in compassion, justice, and good works of mercy, we start by remembering what Christ has already done for us. Lasting change hinges on this inward sanctification. Even if we face trials of many kinds, even if we endure long seasons of suffering, even if we lose *everything*, we have more than enough because we have Christ. And in him, we receive every spiritual blessing. The forgiveness of our sins. God as our Father. Extravagant grace. A guaranteed and glorious inheritance. A future where sorrow ends and unceasing joy begins. This is what kindles our gratitude. We get to know and be known by God. And the more we look *to* him, the more we'll look *like* him.

## Discussion Questions

1. When are you most inclined to feel compassion for others? How can you grow in emulating God's heart of compassion toward both spiritual and physical needs?

2. Do you think anger is ever a godly response to injustice? Why or why not?

3. What expressions of injustice burden your heart? How might God be calling you to confront them? What expressions of injustice are you tempted to either ignore because of apathy or avoid because of controversy?

4. What temptations hinder you from being zealous for good works? How can you foster devotion to good works, even when they're hard?

5. Why is gratitude so crucial to our ability to show mercy to others? What biblical truths or verses might be helpful to meditate on to grow in gratitude for the blessings you've received in Christ?

4

# Orphans and Widows and Sojourners and . . .

WHEN I FIRST BECAME A MOTHER, I was petrified about falling down the steps while holding my newborn son. I was already clumsy, and now the stakes were high. He was so precious and so fragile. I was keenly aware of his helplessness and vulnerability. He depended on my body to feed him and my hands to protect him. As he grew, those worries waned. Of course, I *still* don't want him harmed or hurt. But I don't worry about little things like falling down stairs anymore. He's not vulnerable in the way he used to be.

Our instinct to be careful with the fragile and protective of the weak is a reflection of God's own heart. He made all people in his image and endowed us with unique dignity and worth. We are the crown of his creation. Even the most magnificent mountains and powerful angels don't grab his heart as we do. Isn't that amazing?

Rooted in this love, he has a unique concern for those who are especially weak and vulnerable. Throughout his word, God often references his concern for the fatherless, widows, and sojourners, as well as the broader umbrella of the poor and oppressed. Since God never changes, his concern continues to stretch to these people today. They are precious and valuable in his sight. He's not indifferent to their suffering or denigration. Just as I was extra protective of my newborn son, he's extra protective of those most susceptible to harm.

## Caring for the Fatherless

The whole notion of fatherhood originates with God. It existed eternally within the Trinity and extended into the creation of man. As Father, God has a special tenderness toward the orphan and fatherless. He describes himself as a "helper of the fatherless" and, more intimately, as "father of the fatherless" (Ps. 10:14; 68:5). And he's chosen us—the church—to live as extensions of this love. He cares about their provision and protection. He wants them nurtured and loved.

Children—especially those without parents—face a unique kind of helplessness. Unable to defend themselves, they're at greater risk of abuse. Unable to provide for themselves, they're at greater risk of destitution. This is why the Mosaic law commanded that provisions be made for orphans and why God judged people and nations based on their treatment of the vulnerable. He "executes justice for the fatherless" (Deut. 10:18) and listens attentively to their cry (Ps. 10:18). He also threatens severe punishment to those who mistreat them (Exod. 22:22–24). This is why Psalms instructs, "Give justice to the weak and the fatherless; maintain the right of the afflicted and the destitute. Rescue the weak and the needy; deliver them from the hand of the wicked" (82:3).

James 1:27 is perhaps the most well-known verse about orphan care. It says, "Religion that is pure and undefiled before God the Father is this: to visit orphans and widows in their affliction." Caring for orphans isn't a special or specific calling only to some Christians—it's an essential mark of true religion.

The book of Job illustrates how this correlation has always existed. While being falsely accused by his friends in the midst of his afflictions, Job defended his righteousness by pointing to the fact that he'd helped, fed, and nurtured the fatherless (Job 29:12; 31:17–18). To Job, orphan care was an expected element to living righteously before God. It should be the same for us.

*Getting Practical*

Globally, there are at least 153 million orphans who have lost at least one parent; of those children, over seventeen million are considered "double orphans," having no parents at all.[1] Understanding the difference between these two groups provides valuable insight into the best approaches to orphan care.

Family is God's idea. So whenever possible, we should strive to keep it intact. One reason Scripture specifically addressed fatherlessness is that if children lost their father in Bible times, their mother had little hope of keeping the family afloat. These vulnerabilities still function in many parts of the world today, as women face greater rates of poverty than men and are themselves vulnerable to abuse. Supporting single mothers, then, is vital to caring for the fatherless.

This is one reason well-run sponsorship programs are so effective. Since fatherlessness leads to increases in poverty and

---

1   "On Understanding Orphan Statistics," Christian Alliance for Orphans, June 2015, https://cafo.org/.

vulnerability, some organizations partner with churches to provide resources that not only care for orphans but offer supplemental support to single mothers as well. Sponsorships help cover the costs of food, medical care, and education, helping shoulder the burden of the parent (or caretaker) struggling to provide for her child. Even when children have lost both parents, there may be ways to support their families. Plenty of grandparents, aunts, and uncles desire to care for their orphaned relatives but lack the resources because of their own poverty. When we support them, we care for orphaned children by extension.

Children without relational options are often placed in institutionalized care or end up homeless, exploited, or trafficked, making orphans among the most vulnerable groups in any society.

*Foster Care*

Most children in foster care aren't technically orphans, and extensive efforts are made to reunite them with their families. Foster care isn't just about serving hurting children, but about serving hurting parents—parents who might be struggling because of addiction or mental illness or homelessness or incarceration. Foster care gives parents the gift of time so that they can take the necessary steps to be reunified with their children. It's actually a way of *preventing* orphanhood, by *preserving* the sacred institution of family. When reunification isn't possible, these children effectively become orphans for a season (we'll talk about adoption next).

At any given time, there are roughly four hundred thousand children in the American foster system, and about one hundred thousand of those children are eligible for adoption.[2] All too frequently, siblings are separated, children bounce from home to home, and even the kids who end up in the best foster families bear the sorrow of a life that's been turned upside down. Of the children who age out of foster care without being adopted or reunified with their parents, 20 percent will immediately become homeless, 50 percent will develop substance dependence, 60 percent of young men will be convicted of a crime, less than 3 percent will obtain a college degree, and 25 percent will suffer from post-traumatic stress disorder.[3] When we consider these outcomes, it is obvious that many foster children are left with festering wounds that profoundly affect their futures. Will we—the church—care for them?

Without traditional orphanages in America, it's easy to underestimate the needs here. We may even have a burning passion for orphan care but think of it only in international terms. It's not intentional; it's just the frame of reference we have. Besides, all the unknowns surrounding foster care are daunting. The idea of becoming the primary caretaker of a child who doesn't stay seems unbearable. How is it possible to love children well, while also being willing to let them go? The two *seem* irreconcilable.

I get it. I've felt that way too. I know people who have journeyed into foster care. And while it's true that it's emotionally costly sometimes excruciatingly so—they also showed it was worth it. They've been integral to the vital work of family reunification. They've loved children as their own, advocated for their needs, and

2  Brandon Gaille, "51 Useful Aging Out of Foster Care Statistics: Social Race Media," National Foster Youth Institute, May 26, 2017, https://www.nfyi.org/.

3  Gaille, "51 Useful Aging Out of Foster Care Statistics."

created safe spaces for healing and growth. And because they've loved well, they've lost too.

My best friend Jamie (not to be confused with my other best friend *Jayme*) was a foster mom to "J" for almost *three* years. During that time, she advocated for and supported and encouraged J's biological mom, who was eventually able to bring J home. Even though Jamie was deeply convinced this was the right thing, it was crushing. To keep one family whole, hers was broken.

Entering into such brokenness—the brokenness of families, the brokenness of children, the brokenness of a system—is painful enough to shatter your own heart. But God binds broken hearts, and his grace is sufficient to strengthen and comfort those who engage the ministry of foster care.

But foster parents also get to experience the beautiful too. My brother and sister-in-law were invited to the wedding of their former foster son's mom. He was the adorable ring bearer, she was a beaming bride, and their family had healed and grown in ways they never could have anticipated.

Fostering children is more than just providing a temporary home; it's entering into their pain and tenderly sharing their burdens. Sometimes offering this type of love is met with rejection. Other times it is reciprocated, but that only increases the grief when a deeply loved child leaves. Some parents who foster get to experience the fruit of their labor—they get front-row seats to witness God's healing and transformative power. But many times foster parents do the sowing without getting to reap the harvest. They might spend countless nights rocking a screaming baby who's experiencing substance withdrawal, only to be forgotten once he's reunified with his mother. They might spend months consoling a traumatized child yet never know the healing God brings years later. They might be the one who established a child's ability to attach, only to have someone else enjoy the fruit of attachment.

Without question, foster care carries an intense mix of pain and joy. But there is comfort in this: those who steadfastly pour out their lives for children in foster care can find refuge in *their* good Father. We might lack confidence in our ability, but that drives us to find confidence in his sufficiency. We might fear the future unknowns, but we can cast our fears before his throne. He will be with us.

## Adoption

Throughout history, God has faithfully used Christians to play a pivotal role in orphan care. Until Christ's return—when he brings full restoration and makes all things new—we're called to continue this work. It's important to clarify: the biblical mandate to care for orphans should *not* be considered synonymous with a call to adopt orphans. Christ, our head, has given each member of his body different work to do. But if he loves orphans and sets the solitary in a home, doesn't it make sense that he wants us—the church—providing those homes?

We may not be able to remedy the orphan crisis, but we *can* take action for the accessible number of children who are legally adoptable. There are children *today* waiting to be placed with families, because other avenues to be reunified with biological parents or to find permanent homes have already been exhausted. I pray that someday, rather than thousands of children waiting for parents to adopt them, there would be thousands of parents waiting in line, ready to welcome such children into their families.

Russell Moore writes, "When we adopt—and when we encourage a culture of adoption in our churches and communities—we're picturing something that's true about our God. We, like Jesus, see what our Father is doing and do likewise (John 5:19). And what our Father is doing, it turns out, is fighting for orphans, making them sons and daughters."[4] A hard and holy calling, adoption paints an earthly picture of the gospel.

It's interesting to consider the role adoption played in Jesus's own life. Because of the miracle of the immaculate conception, Jesus wasn't biologically connected to Joseph at all. Even so, Scripture refers to Joseph as Jesus's father. In Matthew's Gospel the genealogy of Jesus is linked through Joseph, even though none of Joseph's blood ran through his veins. Joseph was our Savior's earthly father, solely through adoption.

Not only did adoption mark the beginning of Jesus's life, but it's the reason he came! "When the fullness of time had come, God sent forth his Son, born of woman, born under the law, . . . *so that* we might receive adoption as sons" (Gal. 4:4–5). The good news of the gospel isn't only that we're forgiven of our sins; it's also that we're *adopted* into God's family. Through adoption, we become coheirs with Christ, never to be separated from the love of our Father.

Just as marriage is an earthly picture of Christ's love for the church, adoption is an earthly picture of the gospel. It's because God so loved the world that we've been adopted. We were separated from the Father and utterly helpless to save ourselves. And we weren't just orphans; we were *enemies*—rebels of God and

---

4 Russell D. Moore, *Adopted for Life: The Priority of Adoption for Christian Families and Churches* (Wheaton, IL: Crossway, 2009), 73.

lovers of sin. Still, he had compassion on us. A compassion so strong he paid the greatest price to adopt us as his children. Earthly adoption, then, is just a faint echo of the glorious adoption we receive in Christ.

Adoption mirrors God's pursuit. Just as we're utterly reliant upon the Father's initiative for our own adoption, orphans are reliant upon an adoptive parent. They can't change their state as orphan on their own. Adoption only happens because prospective parents initiate it. They decide when to adopt. They choose where to adopt from. They ensure that all the legal requirements are met. They sign mountains of paperwork and stand before judges and file immigration forms. Adoption never happens by chance—it's consciously pursued.

Adoption also mirrors God's sacrifice. He gave his only Son so that we could be adopted, a far greater sacrifice than we will ever make. But we make real sacrifices too. We give our finances and time and willingly embrace scary unknowns. Some of us absorb the pain of rejection and endure being the target of trauma behaviors. And since we ourselves are sinners, none of this comes easily. We still have to crucify our own flesh and confess our own failings in order to love well.

Finally, adoption mirrors the certainty of our salvation. We aren't partly saved or partly adopted. God doesn't allow us to enter into his family with a lingering threat to kick us out if we don't behave. When we are his, we are his forever. In the same way, my adopted daughter is just as much my child as my biological sons. I'm just as devoted to her as I am to them. Yes, she has another story before entering our family—and we seek to honor her birth mother however we can—but we also remind her that she is completely, unconditionally, and always our daughter. She's not *almost* part of the family—she *is* family. Her place in our family is secure.

These rich theological truths about God's compassion, God's pursuit, God's sacrifice, and the certain adoption *we've received* through Christ are the lens through which we should view adoption. But it's important that we don't romanticize adoption's real-life implications. While adoption is a beautiful part of God's plan, earthly adoption only happens because of brokenness. Poverty, neglect, abandonment, death, loss, and abuse are what make children orphans in the first place. There is tragedy involved—searing pain that only God can heal. Sometimes the "beauty" of adoption is reflecting Christ by loving a child who doesn't reciprocate. Sometimes the "beauty" of adoption is relentlessly trying to convince a child that his or her identity as a son or a daughter is permanent as they struggle to attach because of past neglect. Sometimes the "beauty" of adoption is reflecting Christ's forgiveness, despite being the ongoing target of a child's rage as it erupts from her own sin nature and the unique pain of her past.

Typically, when I consider the beauty of adoption, I think of the happier aspects—an orphan no longer being an orphan but a beloved son or a daughter, with all the rights and benefits that come with a family. But sometimes the beauty of adoption is the intense hardship, just as the beauty of the gospel is only possible because of the great suffering of our Savior.

In addition to demonstrating the gospel and becoming a family to a child who needs one, adoption is a profound way to fulfill the Great Commission. We have the greatest influence for the Lord within our families. When orphans are adopted into Christian families, they are not only loved as sons and daughters but are also given the chance to hear the gospel and witness its transformative power.

Our daughter is from India, where less than 2 percent of the population is Christian, making it unlikely that she'd ever have been exposed to the gospel had she remained there. She lived in a loving—and devoutly Hindu—orphanage. But our girl loves Jesus! We've had the joy of watching her repent of her sins and trust in Christ for her salvation. We've gotten to witness her childlike faith as she brings her heavy burdens to the Lord in prayer and seeks him for refuge. When I see her heart for God, I'm continually struck by the lengths he went to rescue her. He orchestrated a million details so that she'd be adopted into a family where she could hear about him, and ultimately be adopted into *his* family. And because God's heart is for every nation, tribe, and tongue, he leads adoptive families differently. He moves some of us to adopt domestically and others to adopt internationally. He leads some families to adopt children with special needs, some to adopt babies, and others to adopt teens. Every adoption should be celebrated, because every child has eternal value. Adoption isn't just about building an earthly family—it's about introducing our children to the Father, who will never leave or forsake them, so that they can be a part of his everlasting family.

## Caring for Widows

Scripture's emphasis on caring for widows might seem strange to modern, Western thought. Women today can have careers and own property and have success and influence in society. But this wasn't always the case—and in some parts of the world, it still isn't.

In the ancient world, a woman's future was largely at the mercy of her male relatives. So when a woman became a widow, she lost her fundamental source of protection and provision. She became vulnerable to exploitation. If she didn't have a male heir, she lost her property. If you're unfamiliar with the book of Ruth, it tells the story of Ruth and her mother-in-law, Naomi. After Naomi's husband and sons die, Ruth and Naomi are left as destitute widows. Their situation seems hopeless until Boaz honors his role as "kinsman redeemer" and marries Ruth, preserving her and Naomi's future.

As the protector of widows, God called his people to defend and provide for them. They were to ensure that widows received justice. Property owners were commanded to let widows—along with orphans, sojourners, and the poor—glean their fields for food. A portion of the tithe was set aside for their provision. And just as Job exemplified righteousness in how he cared for the orphan, he also showed it by caring for the widow (Job 29:13; 31:18).

In the early church, this remained a priority. Widows were to be honored, and relatives were warned that if they didn't provide for the widows in their own families, they were worse than unbelievers (1 Tim. 5:3–8). Believing women were called to care for their widowed relatives so that the church could focus on those who didn't have families to help them. No widow was to be left behind (1 Tim. 5:16). Church leaders were appointed to ensure the fair distribution of provision among widows because the Hebrews were showing partiality and neglected the Hellenist widows (Acts 6:1–5). Even on the cross, when Jesus prepared to draw his final breath, he made sure his mother, who was likely widowed at the time of his death, would be watched over (John 19:26–27).

Today, many widows still face poverty and are vulnerable to abuse. The church has a crucial role to play: holding Christians accountable to care for their widowed relatives, providing for widows in their congregations, and protecting the dignity of widows in their communities. Even in affluent societies there is need—it's estimated that one in ten people experiences elder abuse in America in a given year.[5] Aside from physical suffering, there is the problem of loneliness. The more isolated and independent our culture becomes, the lonelier we are. Do we take James 1:27 seriously—"Religion that is pure and undefiled before God the Father is this: to visit orphans and widows in their affliction"—not just when it comes to orphans, but when it comes to visiting *widows* in their distress? Loneliness is a real hardship—one that can be severely painful. And we are called, as God's people, to mitigate that pain through our presence.

## The Widows We Shouldn't Overlook

While 1 Timothy 5:3–16 specifically instructs Christians to provide for their widowed relatives and outlines how the church should identify and care for those in their local churches, that doesn't mean we should *limit* our care to these women. God's heart is soft toward widows, and he may give some of us opportunities to reflect his love to other types of widows experiencing loss.

5  "Elder Abuse Statistics," Department of Justice, October 2018, https://www.justice.gov/.

A few months ago, my sister's neighbor was hit by a car and died. His wife and two children were left behind in a flood of shock and grief. They were also left with a half-demolished and unfunctional kitchen. They weren't poor; they were in the middle of a house project. But who can think about finishing a kitchen in a time like that? As people rallied around them, my brother-in-law put his skills to work. He helped finish the kitchen demolition, repaired their hot water heater, and fixed various leaks in the house. My sister took her neighbor's son to school, tended to the family dog, and arranged small get-togethers where the widow could feel comfortable sharing how she was really doing. When Valentine's Day came around, my sister brought over the widow's favorite flowers and treats. Even my ten-year-old niece contributed, always taking the family's trash cans to the curb before trash pickup. Through words and actions and availability and presence, they demonstrated God's heart for this widow and her family.

## Caring for Sojourners

Before we explore our call to love the sojourner, it'll be helpful to review some terms. A *migrant* is someone who temporarily moves from one place to another (such as an exchange student or seasonal laborer). An *immigrant* is someone who comes to live permanently in a foreign country. A *refugee* is someone who's been forced to flee his or her country because of persecution, war, or violence. An *asylum seeker* is similar to a refugee. Asylum seekers pursue sanctuary in another country and then apply for asylum, that is, the right to be recognized as a refugee. They must prove that their fear of persecution in their home country is founded.

While these exact terms aren't used in Scripture, we can find clear parallels. In the Old Testament, the Hebrew term *gēr* translates to "sojourner," "alien," or "stranger," and usually connotes a long-term or resident alien, while the lesser used but related term *tôšāb* "carries with it the sense of a transitory existence within the host community."[6] In the New Testament, the Greek term *xenos* translates to "foreigner" or "stranger."

The use of *gēr* first appears in Genesis 12, when Abram goes to live as an alien in Egypt:

> Abraham from here on is frequently referred to as a "resident alien" (Gen 17:8; 20:1; 21:23, 34: 23:4). Later, the story of Jacob's time in Laban's household (Gen 28–32) is a repetition of this theme as Jacob travels from his land to Paddam Aram. Again Jacob is specifically referred to as a *gēr* in Genesis 28:4 and 32:4. Furthermore, Joseph and the whole clan of Jacob are also designated as aliens in Genesis 47:4 and 9, and four hundred years later Moses identifies himself as an alien through the naming of his son "Gershom," meaning "alien there" (Ex 2:22). Right from the outset the reader clearly recognises that the fathers of Israel experienced an alien identity. Israel's lineage, tradition and self-identity is grounded in the setting of alienation.[7]

Similar themes appear throughout the Bible: Hagar and Ishmael were driven from their home into the desert, where God provided

6    K. J. Tromp, "Aliens and Strangers in the Old Testament," *Vox Reformata* (November 2011): 5.
7    Tromp, "Aliens and Strangers," 15.

for them; Ruth joined Naomi in her return to Israel even though she was a Moabite; David sought asylum in another kingdom when Saul threatened his life; when Herod sought to kill Jesus, Mary and Joseph fled with him to Egypt; and persecution led to the scattering of the early church.

Throughout history, people have sought refuge and relief in foreign lands; throughout history, God has shown his heart to protect and provide for them.

### The Big Picture

There are foundational doctrines undergirding God's heart for the stranger that must impact our own. God created people of every ethnicity and culture as his image bearers. An American person is no more valuable than a person from Mexico or India or Ukraine or China. All our differences reflect *his* creativity and glory. Despite the distance—and sadly, division—that exists between us now, one day people from every tribe and nation will worship Christ in a unified voice (Rev. 7:9–10).

Just as God expressed his heart for orphans and widows in the Old Testament, he reveals his heart for the foreigner too. Most of the moral laws that applied to orphans and widows also applied to sojourners. They had God-given *rights* to glean food and be paid fair wages. A portion of tithe was set aside for their provision, and they were to be included in community celebrations.

I imagine the Israelites had some issues with this. After all, a sojourner wasn't part of God's chosen people. So God reminded them, "You shall not wrong a sojourner or oppress him, for you were sojourners in the land of Egypt" (Exod. 22:21). His instruction didn't end there either. Not only were the Israelites not to harm the sojourner; they were to proactively seek his good: "You shall treat the stranger who sojourns with you as the native among you, and you shall love him as yourself, for you were strangers in the land of Egypt: I am the LORD your God" (Lev. 19:34).

But wait, you might say, we don't live in a theocracy anymore! True. Here's where Job's example helps us yet again. Job was alive well before Israel was established as a nation, and welcoming the sojourner was another evidence of his righteousness (Job 31:32). It's just what God's people do.

Even today, we can identify with immigrants the way the Israelites were reminded to, *because this present world is not our home.* We are just sojourners here, awaiting our King's return. For now, he is still building his kingdom—still seeking and saving those alienated from him—and making for himself a people of every tribe, tongue, and nation.

And he's building this kingdom differently than we'd build ours. We tend to see people's worth based on what they bring to the table. We look at their talent and experience and success. But we've been made citizens of God's kingdom by no merit of our own. God didn't save us based on anything we had to offer, and this truth has massive implications for how we view immigrants. The popular notion of only welcoming the "best and brightest" is staunchly anti-Christian. An immigrant or refugee's worth is not defined by what he can offer. That's not how the kingdom of God works. If our willingness to welcome the stranger rests on his utility, we're expressly defying the heart of our King. We welcome the stranger *because* God welcomed us. We care for the immigrant and the refugee—particularly the *most* vulnerable among them—because that's what our King does.

### Welcome and the Great Commission

God is sovereign over the placement of people. He used persecution to scatter the New Testament church and spread the gospel. Likewise, he continues to use the scattering of Christians *and* unbelievers for the sake of gospel advancement.

According to Pew Research, the US has admitted about 464,700 Christian refugees and about 310,700 Muslim refugees since 2002. The Christians coming here are not only our brothers and sisters in Christ, but our colaborers—they are part of the mission to spread the gospel in America. And most of the Muslim refugees we've received come from countries where there's little to no Christian presence—meaning there's a good chance they've never heard the gospel before. The influx of Muslim refugees, then, is a profound opportunity to fulfill the Great Commission. We cannot neglect it. God has sent us a harvest. Will we labor for it? He's given us a unique opportunity to show his mercy and share the gospel with those who've been oppressed by their own governments and people and religions—people who might be receptive to the gospel for the first time. This also makes them people who will likely experience even more hardship if they convert:

> A church seeking to reach migrants will have to be very aware of this and will have to be ready to enfold and care for new believers who have gone through the traumatic experience of rejection by their communities. The importance of this can-

not be overemphasized. If a migrant community observes a new believer being left to fend for him/herself with little help from the Christian community it will send a powerful negative message to those who might still be considering the claims of Christ. The opposite is also true. A caring Christian community that truly seeks to be the "Body of Christ" can act as a powerful reassurance and witness to those who are perhaps on the cusp of declaring their faith.[8]

When we consider the 89.3 million people worldwide who've been forcibly displaced from their homes, including 27 million who are refugees, it's overwhelming.[9] There's no way we can care for them all. But we aren't supposed to. When we get overwhelmed, it's because we're thinking too broadly. Look for the neighbors closer to home. In the past five years, about two hundred refugees have resettled in my county—which means there are more than enough Christians nearby to care for them all. Consider your own community: Are there local refugees who'd gratefully receive your hand of friendship? Are there ways your church can welcome and serve them? One church in my area hosts weekly ESL classes. Another ran a summer camp for kids. My church has hosted a couple of big picnics for local refugees. We rented a school bus to transport families to our church property for the afternoon, and we provided lunch, played lawn games, talked, laughed over communication struggles, and enjoyed each other's company. It was a beautiful time of fellowship

8    Phillip Scheepers, "Migration: An Opportunity for the Gospel," *Vox Reformata* (November 2011): 82.
9    "Figures at a Glance," UN Refugee Agency, June 16, 2022, https://www.unhcr.org/.

with believers who'd fled persecution and of intentional connection with Muslim families. Best of all, some lasting relationships were formed.

### The Importance of Identity

When considering the sojourner, it's vital to remember our core identity. We're Christians before we're Americans (or whatever nationality you are). Though we were strangers of God, he paid a great cost to make us his people. Do you see strangers—even those who have nothing to offer—and love them? Do you look for ways to welcome them? Or do you view them as unnecessary burdens on society?

Our response to these questions has serious implications. In the chilling passage of the final judgment, Jesus separates the sheep from the goats—those who are truly his people and those who aren't. And one of the distinguishing marks was their response to strangers. Those who didn't welcome them were punished; those who welcomed them were rewarded (Matt. 25:31–46).

We'll discuss the importance of hospitality in a later chapter, but one important detail to note is that the Greek word used in the New Testament for hospitality is *philoxenia*, which means "love of strangers." True hospitality isn't just about blessing family and friends—it's about loving strangers.

And this call goes past our own homes. As God's people we have a part to play in creating a culture that welcomes the stranger. We should care about how immigrants are treated in public places. We should want them paid fairly for their work. We should support those who are trying to assimilate. It's difficult to live in a foreign country. Are we patient and kind when cultural expectations collide? Do we need to repent of using or tolerating dehumanizing slurs? This is particularly important to consider regarding undocumented immigrants. We're called to love and value strangers *regardless of their legal status*. Human dignity doesn't rest on documentation.

Of course, immigration policies are complex and complicated to address. It's not in the purview of this book to discuss the ins and outs of what reform should look like. You and I don't have much control over those things anyway. But while policies are complicated, our calling isn't—we must value sojourners as fellow image bearers of God and treat them with an ethic of love.

## The Poor and Oppressed

We've already considered three specific groups in Scripture—the widow, the fatherless, and the sojourner. But God paints a broader stroke too.

Let's take one last look at our righteous friend Job. The guy's daily life was marked by righteousness and justice (Job 29:14). He delivered the poor who cried for help, aided the blind and lame, and defended the helpless (29:12, 15, 17). Job couldn't bear the thought of ignoring needs he was able to meet. With a flair for the dramatic, he even said that if he was found guilty of doing so, "then let my shoulder blade fall from my shoulder, and let my arm be broken from its socket" (31:16–22).

Why this intensity? Because Job feared God, he was appalled at the thought of neglecting God's image bearers. Will we share his passion? Will we see what God sees and care for those God cares about? Though the ways in which poverty and oppression manifest today are too many to count, let's skim a few examples.

Almost 10 percent of the global population experiences hunger.[10] God sees those suffering due to famine and poverty and corruption. He sees the parents who sacrifice their own meals to feed their sons and daughters. He sees the malnourished and their distended stomachs. He sees the laborer left without money to pay for his food. God sees and cares and wants to use his people to nourish them (Isa. 58:10).

A staggering 30 percent of women and girls worldwide have experienced either physical or sexual violence.[11] God grieves violence against women and girls. From the all too common practice of gendercide—the killing of unborn and baby girls—to the rampant abuse against women, God hates it all. Because of the normalcy of such denigration, the church must be on the front lines defending and affirming the value of women.

The majority of babies prenatally diagnosed with Down Syndrome are aborted,[12] and children with physical and intellectual impairments are three to four times more likely to experience abuse than nondisabled children.[13] All over the world, people with disabilities are abandoned, discriminated against, treated as worthless, and robbed of education and opportunity. God sees those who suffer because of disabilities—the precious lives that are mistreated, considered cursed, and ostracized from society. May

10   "World Hunger: Key Facts and Statistics 2022," Action Against Hunger, https://www
     .actionagainsthunger.org/.
11   "Violence against Women," World Health Organization, March 9, 2021, https://www
     .who.int/.
12   Sarah Zang, "The Last Children of Down Syndrome," *The Atlantic*, December 2020,
     https://www.theatlantic.com/.
13   "Children with Disabilities," UN Special Representative of the Secretary-General on
     Violence Against Children, United Nations, accessed January 9, 2023, https://violence
     againstchildren.un.org/.

the church stand apart. When disability is met with mistreatment, let us rush to defend. When disability induces pain, let us bring comfort. When disability yields poverty, let us offer provision. When disability causes isolation, let us give friendship.

Those whom society has deemed weak and worthless and unlovely must know of the Savior who is acquainted with grief, a Savior who himself was rejected so that they could be accepted and redeemed.

## One Savior for All

*I had no idea.* This thought has echoed in the chambers of my heart countless times. It seems there is no end to the devastating facets of human suffering. We haven't even addressed the pervasiveness of persecution, racism, human trafficking, and exploitive labor practices. We haven't reviewed scores of data surrounding preventable diseases, lack of healthcare, and water-borne illnesses. We haven't discussed natural disasters and wars and the havoc they cause.

It's a lot. And to be perfectly honest, it often leads me to despair. In some ways, despair seems inevitable. If we're cultivating hearts of compassion, we'll grieve the afflictions wrought by injustice and poverty. If we're committed to good works of mercy, we'll lament how our efforts can barely cause a ripple in an ocean of problems. Because of this, Christian growth in mercy often introduces the coinciding temptation to feel hopeless and question the goodness of God.

Some of my darkest periods of spiritual struggle have occurred when I've been most invested in mercy ministry. When grappling with the adversity many endure, my finite mind finds it difficult to reconcile such misery with the sovereignty of God. The promise of heaven and eternal communion with Christ is greatly reassuring when I consider the suffering of the saints, but such contemplation offers no comfort when faced with the afflictions of the unsaved. Besides the struggles that spring from my own heart, I also have an enemy who wants to pervert godly pursuits of justice and mercy to drive me away from God. Satan wants to render us useless for the mission, and what greater sadistic strategy can he employ than to manipulate our kingdom work to make us question our King?

This is why it's imperative to continually guard our hearts and minds in Scripture, clinging to the truths we know of God's character. He *is* good. He *is* just. He *is* faithful and merciful and wise. During times of deep despair, studying the attributes of God always encourages me. Beholding his beauty and perfection reminds me that the darkness that exists is the result of living in a fallen world filled with sinful people. God created a beautiful paradise to be enjoyed, and it was sin that plagued the world with disease and disaster. God is the source of all righteousness, goodness, mercy, and justice. It was sin that birthed hate, violence, greed, and corruption. All the suffering and evil we see shouldn't drive us away but rather point us to the only one who redeems the broken and purifies the wretched. Jesus Christ is the only hope we have and the only lasting hope we can offer.

**Discussion Questions**

1. Why is a robust understanding of the *imago Dei*—the truth that *all* people are made in the image of God—crucial to valuing people as God does? What are some examples of ways the world denigrates human worth? In what ways are you tempted to?

2. Read Matthew 25:31–46. This passage illustrates that God's people don't just avoid evil but actively tend to the needs of others. Why is Jesus giving this sober warning? How should we respond to it?

3. From Job to the Israelites to the New Testament church, we've seen how God's people are called to care for widows, orphans, sojourners, and the poor and oppressed. In what ways are you currently obeying that call? How would you like to grow?

4. We all fail. How does the gospel help us experience conviction without condemnation?

5. Which of God's attributes do you struggle to remember or believe when burdened by the suffering in our fallen world? What verses are helpful to meditate on when feeling discouraged?

5

# The Power of Words

ON NOVEMBER 8, 2018, one of the most disastrous wildfires in California history began. For seventeen days, a fire of raging flames consumed every- and anything in its path—ninety people were killed, and over 18,800 structures were damaged. Most of the destruction occurred in the first four hours. When James 3 compares the tongue to an unruly flame, this is what we should picture. Our words have far more power than we realize, able to do more damage than we can imagine. We must wield them carefully.

Yet for all this danger, our words also have the capacity for much good, because death *and* life are in the power of the tongue (Prov. 18:21). The entire universe was birthed into existence by the voice of God (Gen. 1:1–27). Esther's petition saved her people from certain death (Est. 7:3–4). The woman at the well testified to her town that Jesus was the Messiah (John 4:28–29). And with the cry, "It is finished," the victory of God's mercy-filled mission was secured (John 19:30).

Because of Jesus's triumphant words, our words can be sanctified—set ablaze to ignite God's glory and goodness to the world.

## Power to Pray

Prayer is the simplest and most powerful way to be doers of mercy. We are limited in our reach and resources, but God isn't. We can't bring rain to relieve famine, but he can. We can't change the hearts of kings or the plans of rulers, but he can. We can't heal the sick or mend the brokenhearted, but he can. We can't bring dead sinners to life, but he can. He is never thwarted by wicked dictators or destructive laws. He is never confused or overwhelmed or unable to act. He uplifts the weak and needy. He is a Father to the fatherless and a defender of widows. He has compassion on his children and attends to their cry. He delights to save the lost. We should lift our voices with confidence because our almighty God hears us.

When the brokenness of this world burns on our hearts and tempts us to despair, we must remember who rules over everything and pray. We may feel overwhelmed by the scope of human suffering and frustrated by our inability to mend it, but God isn't. While we wring our hands in worry, his sovereign hands remain unshaken. And with powerful precision, his will prevails. God hasn't designed prayer as a last resort—that practice we do because our hands are tied. It's meant to be our first, middle, and final course of action.

Prayer helps us place our hope in God rather than in ourselves. It acknowledges his lordship and our limitations. It reminds us that he is the sovereign one and doesn't, in fact, depend on us. What good news! The world is too broken a place to try to carry on our own shoulders. We must go back to God, again and again, trusting him to renew it. As we lift our words to him, he lifts our hearts from despair and strengthens us for service.

The hard reality of prayer is that it confronts our self-sufficient tendencies. We want to fix problems ourselves. Prayer doesn't feel very involved when we intercede for the souls of the unsaved. Prayer doesn't feel like the most effective way to be a doer of justice. When we pray, we lack that sense of accomplishment or progress that we might experience with deeds of mercy. It's not about us though; it's about God being at work. We aren't the answer to the world's problems. He is.

Through prayer, the Spirit also changes our own hearts, increasing our compassion for the spiritual and physical state of others. By praying for specific people and specific needs, our hearts become invested in them. We grow sensitive to the Spirit and start to realize ways he's called us to respond to some of those prayers. It's by praying for the hungry that we remember to share with them. It's by praying for the lonely that we remember to pursue them.

Since we don't always witness the results of our prayers, they tend to feel useless. Yet God is always working, and we can trust him for what we can't see. But every so often, God graciously allows us to witness the fruit of our prayers. One of my favorite recollections of this was discovering how my friend Sandy's prayers intertwined with mine, and how they were both answered.

Sandy is an education counselor. She's not only dedicated to helping students in their education but also carries their spiritual well-being on her heart. She regularly prays for them and entrusts her petitions to God, knowing she probably won't see the outcome. One time she met a young refugee student who'd just resettled in America and been diagnosed with autism. The culmination of his diagnosis, war-related family trauma, and lack of English made his an especially complicated case. When Sandy became aware of his younger siblings and another sibling on the way, her burden for this family became even more pronounced.

One day at church, she expressed her heart to my mom. Though she only shared general details, my mom realized that the situation Sandy described sounded familiar. After bringing me into the conversation, we discovered that the family Sandy had spent months praying for was the *same* family I'd just started visiting through volunteer work. Long before I began praying for God to provide a caring advocate at this child's school, Sandy—a caring advocate at school—had already been praying for him. Our gracious God heard and answered her prayers. He also moved others to bring meals, buy groceries, and send gifts when the new baby was born. At a time when this refugee family was completely disconnected from their own family and recovering from significant crisis and transition, God worked through Sandy's prayers to care for them.

God is always faithful to listen, so we must be faithful to pray. Take stock of your prayer habits. How often do you incorporate prayer for the lost, the poor, and the oppressed into your life? When you see a tragic headline, do you pray? When you encounter a person in need, do you pray? When you learn of a disease outbreak, a war, a child abused, a family displaced, a shooting, or any number of troubling situations, do you pray? The more consistently we practice prayer, the more natural it becomes.

Too often, the focus of my prayers has rested on me and my actions, and I've neglected prayerful intercession for others. I pray that *I* grow in generosity, that *I* grow in mercy, and that *I* share the gospel boldly. Those are important things to pray for, but I tend to forget to pray for the ministries we support, for my unsaved friends, and for the persecuted church. My instinct toward others is almost always action over prayer. But when my heart is heavy, my first response should be to petition my God. Prayer must be our reflex, not our fallback.

Because prayer isn't always our instinctual response, it's helpful to plan specific times for intercession. Good intentions are useless when we don't take practical steps to follow through. We need to build habits. After months of wanting—and failing—to pray consistently as a family, buying a whiteboard was a game-changer. I listed out a prayer schedule and hung it above our dinner table. On "Mission Monday," we pray for the ministry partners we financially support. On "The Great Commission Tuesday," we pray for the global spread of the gospel and the salvation of unsaved friends. On "Widow and Orphan Wednesday," we pray for the widowed nannies from my daughter's orphanage and children in need of families. "Suffering People Saturday" is a catchall that allows us to rotate prayers for various groups. On these days we might pray for refugees, victims of trafficking, or those affected by a recent natural disaster. The simple step of writing a schedule on a whiteboard dramatically transformed our family prayer habits. I only wish I had done it years ago.

It's also helpful to use certain times of the day as "prayer prompts." We can pray during our commutes to work, when we mow the lawn, or while we feed our babies. Ever since getting a dog, I go on multiple walks each day. I still enjoy podcasts and audiobooks during these walks, but I try to commit at least one daily walk to prayer.

We should also be intentional to pray together, because prayer was never meant to be a solely solitary practice. By committing to pray with our children, alongside our friends, and during church, we'll stir one another's compassion for others and confidence in God to work.

## Power to Preach

Our works of mercy are meant to point to the greatest mercy ever shown. Good works *amplify* the good news. And we need to remember this crucial connection because we all share the same ultimate need: forgiveness of sins and reconciliation with God. More than refugees need safety, they need refuge in Christ. More than orphans need family, they need to be adopted as God's children. More than the poor need food, they need the bread of life. Our acts of service are like an illustration, helping others understand God's story of redemption. But an illustration alone isn't enough—stories must have words.

One reason we're hesitant to preach the gospel is our own insecurity. We trip up over our words. We use too much "Christianese," language that makes sense to us but not to the unbelievers we encounter. We want to make the gospel understandable without compromising it. We know we lack eloquence and persuasiveness. But Scripture offers hope to counter those fears. We can say with Paul, "I am not ashamed of the gospel, for it is the power of God for salvation to everyone who believes" (Rom. 1:16). God doesn't rely on our delivery to accomplish his purposes; the power isn't in the eloquence of our words, but in the truth of his words. It is the gospel that is the power of salvation.

Throughout history God has used weak and unimpressive people to spread the good news. In the book of Acts, he caused *explosive* growth in the church through the bold proclamation of common people. Peter and John's influence confounded the scribes and high priests: "When they saw the boldness of Peter and John, and perceived that they were uneducated, common men, they were astonished" (Acts 4:13). By any earthly standard, Peter and John weren't remarkable. They were simple men—no advanced degrees or doctorates. But they intimately knew and boldly testified to an amazing Savior. The same God who worked through them can work through us too.

God doesn't depend on our eloquence. He simply calls us to know him, to love him, and to unleash his word. He's the one who accomplishes saving work. We are merely ambassadors, sent to spread his fame among every nation, tribe, and tongue. When we share the gospel, it is *his* power that brings the dead to life and melts the heart of stone. Remembering this bolsters our confidence and crucifies our pride.

## Power to Teach

The Great Commission instructs that we not only spread the gospel but that we teach others to follow *all* that Christ has commanded (Matt. 28:20). This includes what he's taught about compassion, justice, and deeds of mercy.

You don't have to be a pastor, small-group leader, or seminary student to play a role in discipleship. Jesus equips each of us to teach others in some degree. As we live as humble students of him and his word, we're entrusted to impart what we learn to others. Discipleship is a shared Christian responsibility, a way we collectively labor for the health of the whole body.

Comprehensive discipleship is essential for growth. This is why pastors must faithfully instruct on biblical mercy and justice—so that fruit grows in the soil of sound doctrine rather than the malformed messages of our culture. But outside of pastoral responsibility, we can all teach others through the capacities God has given us. As the Spirit transforms and teaches us, we can encourage others to pursue Christ instead of comfort, mercy instead of materialism, and service instead of selfishness.

Many Christians struggle to practice mercy, not because they don't want to but because they just don't know how. Merciful believers multiply by teaching others about mercy. So as we learn practical ways to implement these biblical imperatives, we edify the body by teaching about them. Those with experience caring for the homeless can share about the challenges and successes in order to help others discern how to get involved. Those with experience navigating the complexities of immigration law can help others cultivate a more informed, compassionate, and nuanced view of immigration.

In our church, the amount of families involved in the ministry of foster care has rapidly grown over the past several years. One way God has stirred this growth is through foster families sharing their experiences with others. As scary unknowns become worthwhile risks and as faceless statistics transform into beloved children, a passion for foster care spreads. Mercy has a domino effect.

One reason believers are called to meet together is to stir one another up to love and good works (Heb. 10:24). I'm so easily preoccupied with my own circumstances, but when I fellowship with friends and hear how they're caring for their hurting neighbors, it stirs me up to love and good works. I am moved not only by their example but also by what they teach me. We can all make assumptions about *why* a person (or people group) is suffering—or have a narrow view of how to help him. We're all limited in our experiences, expertise, and perspectives. We *need* to learn from others. Over the years, I've benefited so much from those who challenged my assumptions and helped me better process particular issues through a wholistic—and more biblical—lens.

Just as it's important to teach one another in our church communities, it's important to instruct those in our households. Parents have a particular influence in teaching their children to love mercy and live missionally. A large part of how our children view themselves and others comes from us. For better or worse, we're always teaching. Always influencing. So we must consider, are we teaching them to honor the *imago Dei* in all people and discipling them to be doers of mercy? Are we teaching them God's heart of compassion and justice? Are we helping them to "go and do likewise," or are we sheltering them from seeing—or considering—those in need?

Of course we need discernment in how to do this. We should consider our children's ages, emotional maturity, personal struggles, and even past trauma. Knowing that my daughter has to process her own adoption story, I need to be careful in how I discuss the orphan crisis in India. As parents, God has entrusted us to protect our kids, but part of protecting them is preparing them. It is far better to incrementally help our children process through the evil and suffering of the world than to shelter them from it and set them up for faith-shaking surprise later on. The problem of evil is a common stumbling block to faith. My own deepest faith crisis occurred when I was entrenched in learning about child sex-trafficking in Cambodia. As difficult as it is, we *need* to foster an awareness of suffering and oppression in order to help our children process our broken world through the lens of Scripture. We need to teach them that while suffering is pervasive, our Savior will ultimately triumph over it. Racism, human trafficking, persecution, hunger, and abuse may persist now, but someday, Jesus will return as a victorious king and set everything right.

## Power to Speak Up

You know the verse. It regularly makes its rounds on social media and is used on all sorts of products. My very favorite sweatshirt actually has its familiar words printed on it: "Speak up for those who cannot speak for themselves, for the rights of all who are destitute. Speak up and judge fairly; defend the rights of the poor and needy" (Prov. 31:8–9 NIV).

Many of us have been given certain blessings, privileges, and influence that aren't afforded to others. Some of us were born into loving families where hard work was modeled, education was valued, and spiritual health was nurtured. Some of us had parents who paid for our college tuition, or at least drove us to our jobs so we could. Some of us have privileges we fail to recognize because of the color of our skin or the area where we live. Some of us haven't faced major injustices or hurdles that others have faced. In itself, that's not necessarily something to feel guilty about. I'm grateful I grew up in circumstances that taught me I had a voice and gave me the power to use it. But my experience isn't universal. Some people are abused and steamrolled and taken advantage of and manipulated and mistreated and aren't able to defend themselves. When they try to use their voice, it's muted, ignored, or dismissed. We need to recognize this and realize that our own voices aren't meant to be solely used for our own well-being. God's good gifts are never intended to culminate in the cul-de-sacs of our lives but to overflow into the lives of others. Any measure of privilege or influence we have should be leveraged for the good of others.

When we don't face a certain type of discrimination, we're responsible to stand up for those who do. When we aren't oppressed in a particular way, we're responsible to stand up for those who are. Proverbs instructs, "Do not withhold good from those to whom it is due, when it is in your power to do it" (Prov. 3:27). Wherever it is we have a voice, we must use it to speak for those who don't.

To put this into practice, we need to discern our areas of influence and opportunities to speak up. It might look like a man speaking up for a woman being harassed on public transportation because she wears a hijab. It could be a student defending a classmate who's bullied because of his disability, or a pediatrician calling child services when she observes signs of abuse against a patient.

Whatever the situation, speaking up is hard. Even nerve-wracking. I'll never forget watching an airplane passenger grab a flight attendant's waist and shove her so forcefully out of his way that she almost fell over. Surrounding witnesses expressed sympathy, but nobody spoke up on her behalf. After an internal battle, adrenaline coursed through my veins as I finally walked the aisle to confront him. My words fell on deaf ears and he attempted to justify his aggressive behavior, citing that he was a paying customer and she was in his way. I can't remember how many times I repeated, "It doesn't matter. You can't shove a woman." It was a fruitless and blood-boiling encounter. But when I got back to my seat, the flight attendant hugged and thanked me. It served as a key reminder that even when speaking up doesn't fix problems, it comforts those who've been hurt by them. It shows that we see. It shows that we care.

To effectively speak up, we must put our words to work—at least, when possible. As the saying goes, actions speak louder than words. It's easy to talk a big talk without practicing what we preach. We might speak up for the unborn, but do we show practical care to the mother in crisis? We might speak up for refugees, but do we bother reaching out to those who've resettled nearby? We might speak up against racism, but do we ask the Spirit to reveal ways we're blind to our own prejudice? Our actions should validate our words; otherwise we fool ourselves into thinking we care about a myriad of issues without actually being willing to embrace any amount of personal sacrifice or discomfort to address them.

Despite its many dangers and flaws—and the sordid way it fuels today's outrage culture—social media *can* be a useful tool for speaking up and stirring action. As I write, Ukraine remains under attack by Russia. A friend of mine has relationships with people who live there. As they've shared stories from "on the ground" she's spread them on social media, along with information regarding specific ways to help. As my friend continues speaking up for those under siege, she's stirring a response—and honestly, I've found that far more compelling than any news outlet.

Though I've seen my share of carnage on social media, I've witnessed pretty miraculous fruit too. As you've probably picked up by now, I'm a passionate advocate for refugees. I regularly use social media to share international news, immigration updates, and compelling articles. When there are specific opportunities to aid refugee families living in my area, I spread the word. One refugee family I know has endured severe health challenges. When the father underwent major heart surgery, I shared a Facebook fundraiser with the aim of raising enough money to cover a month's rent while he recovered—it *took only eight hours to reach that goal.* And that was just by tapping into my circle of Facebook friends. They saw a need and responded generously (it's important to note that this included friends with differing political views on refugee resettlement).

We can be more than just a voice. We can take ownership and point others to take ownership, to pray, give, love, and serve people whose voices aren't being heard.

### Humility and Boldness

It seems like everything is a hot-button issue these days. Even in the church, we're quick to label each other, make premature judgments, and speak before we listen. This is particularly true regarding issues of injustice. If I say "racism" or "sexism" or "pro-life" or "immigration" or "social justice," assumptions follow. Instead of trying to understand each other—instead of asking, "Can you explain what you mean?"—we see who can yell the loudest. We make straw-man arguments and misrepresent those who think differently from us. We're quick to counter any issue with the deflective question, "What about_____?" as if two things can't be true or lamentable at the same time. We need to stop. "Let every person be quick to hear, slow to speak, slow to anger" (James 1:19).

Christians, of all people, should embody humility when discussing various manifestations of brokenness in this world. We know that sin is insidious, so we should never be surprised by injustice and corruption. And because sin is so insidious, we should never oversimplify how to address it.

We should *all* value the sanctity of human life (from womb to tomb), we should *all* oppose the sins of racism and sexism, we should *all* seek justice and love mercy—yet we're going to have different perspectives and opinions on how to do that. And it's a good thing, because usually these problems are best addressed through a variety of angles.

Because so many of these heated social issues are complicated, Christians must be committed to charitable judgments and reasonable discourse. By *reasonable*, I don't mean noncommittal or weak. To truly honor the *imago Dei* in all people, there are certain truths we can't flounder over. We can't always "agree to disagree."

Charles Spurgeon is one of the most famous and influential preachers in history. He's known for his love of God, passion for the gospel, evangelistic fervor, and fidelity to Scripture. If there was ever a guy who could be called Christ-centered or gospel-centered, it was he. Yet, he was also an outspoken opponent of slavery and racism. He knew the gospel impacted every area of life—that Christ not only saves us from the damnation of sin but also calls us to turn from it. And in his day, the blatant sins of slavery and racism were widely tolerated in the church. He may be known as "the prince of preachers" now, but he wasn't welcome to preach in *many* American churches because of his stand. If he were still alive, I wonder how many people would label him as "woke" or as a "social justice warrior" or at least guilty of distracting from the gospel. But it was Spurgeon's very passion for the gospel that motivated him to speak up against oppression.

Following Spurgeon's example, we can't let fear of conflict cause us to disengage from controversy. Instead, we must ask God to sanctify our engagement. He can help us speak with boldness *and* gentleness, with truth *and* grace. This is crucial because self-righteousness and arrogance toward others always grieve God, even when we're "right" about something. I'm writing this book because I'm passionate about pursuing mercy and justice for the sake of the mission. Since you picked it up, I'm guessing you are too. But I think there's a warning for us. Sin has a way of poisoning good fruit. We can easily become "mercy and justice" pharisees, harshly judging those who seem—at least by our assessment—lacking in this area. We tend to think of pharisees as those who clutch their pearls in disgust at some "unseemly" behavior, the type of people who sneer at unwed pregnant mothers and raise their eyebrows at the heavily tattooed teen walking into church. But we're *all* tempted toward self-righteousness, and there is more than one way to be a pharisee. If I feel contempt toward Christians who don't seem to "get it," I need to remember how much my own sin grieves God. Every one of us has blind spots, and we all need the Spirit's help—and each other's—to change. It is God's kindness that leads us to repentance, so we must bear with one another patiently and only bring correction in love. We can trust our Savior to finish the good work he started.

Jesus commands our words to be seasoned with salt. As anyone who cooks knows, salt is an essential ingredient to most good dishes. It amplifies natural flavors and accentuates spices. Imagine that "truth" is the main course. Without salt—or grace—it will be tasteless and undesirable to eat. But with too much salt—that is, grace at the expense of truth—it's impossible to decipher the flavors of the actual meal because the salt overpowers everything else. It ruins the entire dinner. Words that are palatable always involve the combination of truth and grace. Our only power of persuasion lies in the ability to present them with a kindness that does not compromise conviction—sweetness of speech increases persuasiveness (Prov. 16:21).

Speaking up requires boldness and a willingness to face potential conflict. Too often, fear of controversy prevents Christians from speaking into arenas where the truth of Scripture is strangely absent. We might believe in the sanctity of human life beginning at conception, but we're so scared of being demonized that we refrain from speaking about it at all. We might justify such silence by claiming that confronting abortion will hurt our witness (thanks to the hateful pro-life groups we might get lumped into). It certainly can if we lack grace, but that doesn't negate our responsibility to speak up for those who cannot speak for themselves. These little ones—whom the Creator of the heavens and the earth saw fit to knit together—are worthy of protection. We cannot minimize their worth by remaining silent about their death.

The need to face controversy is also true regarding the issue of racism. Whether attributable to apathy, ignorance, or downright denial, it's troubling how common it is for white Christians to ignore or dismiss problems of ongoing racism. The usual defense: *People are too easily offended these days. Discussing racism just stirs more division. This issue is a distraction from the gospel.* Meanwhile, we ignore many of our own brothers and sisters in Christ. The sins of pride and partiality—the entangling roots of racism—have been temptations in the church since its birth. Given the vise grip it had on our nation, *including* many American churches, for centuries, it's naïve to assume the tentacles of racism aren't still present in our society and congregations today. Sin is pervasive, insidious, and subtle. We should neither deny nor despair when it rears its ugly head. Instead, we can run to our Savior, trusting his power to crush it.

Christians are called to put on humility, no matter the shade of our skin. But may I plead a minute with my white brothers and sisters in Christ? I urge you to *listen* to people of color—particularly fellow believers. There are many God-fearing, gospel-loving, Bible-believing Christians speaking to the issue of racism who can help us see and engage it in light of Scripture. Learn from their wisdom and perspectives and then amplify their voices to those who might otherwise ignore them. If more of us were humble to listen, prayerful to consider, eager to grow, and bold to discuss this controversial topic, we could take greater strides toward true unity.

## A Time for Silence, a Time to Speak

"When words are many, transgression is not lacking, but whoever restrains his lips is prudent" (Prov. 10:19). I need to remember this verse more often. Most likely, you do too. We need to practice restraint. There are times that call for silence—for listening ears and quiet spirits. Times of pause and reflection. Restraining our lips is crucial to using them. If we want our words to be life-giving and fruitful and persuasive, we must learn to quiet them first.

However, sometimes we mistakenly view our silence as a stoic display of self-control because we feel we know better than to stir disunity. But perpetual silence over issues of injustice accomplishes absolutely nothing to build unity. Instead, it communicates that an issue isn't worth caring about, which communicates that the people affected aren't people worth caring about. This attitude is what distracts from the gospel.

Whether we're talking about unborn babies, unarmed Black men, undocumented immigrants, or a myriad of other controversial topics, by failing to speak up we are buying the same lie that perpetuates injustice against them—that only certain lives have value and are worth protecting. Oh, God, forgive us! We also might justify silence because we speak up about other and less controversial injustices, but I found this quote an apt challenge to such a notion:

> If I profess with the loudest voice and clearest exposition every portion of the truth of God except precisely that little point which the world and the devil are at the moment attacking, I am not confessing Christ, however boldly I may be professing Christ. Where the battle rages there the loyalty of the soldier is proved, and to be steady on all the battlefield besides is mere flight and disgrace if he flinches at that point.[1]

So, yes, speak up for all who are oppressed, but don't neglect complex or unpopular justice issues out of fear of controversy.

Silence sometimes feels like the moral high ground, but many times it isn't. Sometimes our silence reflects that we are more callous than compassionate and more concerned with preserving superficial peace than pursuing genuine justice. If we are to

---

1   Martin Luther, in John Piper, *Contending for Our All: Defending Truth and Treasuring Christ in the Lives of Athanasius, John Owen, and J. Gresham Machen* (Wheaton, IL: Crossway, 2006), 36.

imitate the compassionate character of God, If we are to live in love for our neighbors, we must speak up.

## Discussion Questions

1. What are your current prayer habits? How can you incorporate prayer for the lost and suffering into your rhythms of prayer?

2. Good works are essential to our Christian witness, but they're not enough. Why must we *tell* others the good news of the gospel? When was the last time you shared this good news with an unbeliever?

3. We noted that merciful believers multiply by teaching others about mercy. Who can you teach? Who can you learn from?

4. In what situations might God be leading you to speak up for someone else? How can you grow in engaging controversial justice issues with humility? How can you grow in boldness?

5. Why should Christian speech be marked by grace and truth? What are you marked by?

# 6

# The Mission of Money

I FORGOT TO GIVE MY HUSBAND a present for his thirty-fifth birthday. Or a card. Or anything. It's worth noting that *my* birthday was only two weeks before, and he'd gotten me a beautiful woven hammock. He's a gracious guy though, so rather than resenting me, it's become a running joke. But what if it hadn't been a mistake—what if I *never* gave gifts to my husband while happily purchasing things for myself? You'd probably question how much I loved him.

The way we use our money says a lot about what—and who—we love. It reveals the true treasure of our hearts. Perhaps this is why it's so uncomfortable to talk about. It feels too exposing. That discomfort is actually an expression of God's grace to us. He wants us to love what he loves—he exposes our hearts so that they can be refined. There's a reason Jesus spoke more about money and possessions than heaven and hell combined. He wants us to follow him, and following him can't be separated from giving. Jesus showed his love by giving his life. He became poor so we might become rich. He emptied himself so we could be filled. He died so we could live.

If God's love truly abides in us, we will love in both word and deed—it's impossible to do otherwise. We won't close our hearts but will lay down our lives to generously tend to those in need. If this fruit is lacking, Scripture questions whether the love of God is in us at all. First John 3:16–18 says:

> By this we know love, that he laid down his life for us, and we ought to lay down our lives for the brothers. But if anyone has the world's goods and sees his brother in need, yet closes his heart against him, how does God's love abide in him? Little children, let us not love in word or talk but in deed and in truth.

The *primary* purpose of our money is about loving God and our neighbors, and giving generously transforms our money into a pleasing sacrifice of worship. But like Cain, we tend to give our leftovers instead of our best. The idols of materialism and financial security beckon us to feed their insatiable appetites and undermine the priority of generosity. If we're wealthy and successful, we're tempted to buy superfluous things and save far more than we need. If we're frugal and financially stressed, we're tempted to live anxiously tightfisted and trust ourselves more than God to provide. Whatever our situation, living generously goes against our flesh. But it's possible, because we've been made new.

Because of Christ's generous grace to us, we can live generously toward others. And as we sacrifice for the sake of mercy, we'll reap abundant joy. It really is more blessed to give than to receive.

## Common Hindrances to Generosity

Whether living amidst poverty or plenty, the temptation to idolize money and possessions is universal. Living in a prosperous society accentuates this enticement, as culture fuels our fleshly yearnings to believe we need more, deserve more, and should pursue more. In order to embrace the mission of our money, we must first learn to identify and fight the most common temptations we face.

### Hindrance #1: Subtle Acceptance of a "Prosperity Gospel"

There is a common false teaching that's infiltrated the church—the idea that if we love God and have enough faith, we'll be blessed with health, wealth, and prosperity. Many of us reject this "prosperity gospel." We know the real gift of the gospel is knowing Christ—that true abundance is found in loving and being loved by him.

And yet, even when we're grieved by this twisted "gospel," we allow it to subtly infiltrate our hearts. Sometimes we do this by confusing presumption with faith. Faith is following and trusting God through the hard circumstances he ordains; it's not pursuing lifestyles we can't afford or taking on loans we cannot responsibly repay because we "trust" God to provide for our discontented appetites. There will be plenty of opportunities throughout our lives to exercise faith and trust God for provision; we shouldn't create them by allowing our own presumption to cause unnecessary financial strain.

Another subtle way we might embrace prosperity thinking is in how we view God's gifts. It is tempting to assume that we deserve certain possessions, lifestyles, and experiences. We set expectations based on those around us, following norms within the culture without recognizing how much it's caused us to compromise Christ's own warnings to not store up treasures on earth. We might think, "I work diligently and serve God. Of course there's nothing wrong with using my hard-earned money to feed my desires, just as long as I give thanks and acknowledge it's from him." Yes, *God does give good gifts for us to enjoy!* And in his mysterious sovereignty, he gives some of us more than others. Disparity in wealth *isn't* inherently sinful, and neither is enjoying God's gifts. Scripture actually warns us against the false religious practice of asceticism (Col. 2:18–23). But sometimes our "enjoyment" of God's gifts is a flashing indicator of selfishness and greed, if we neglect the poor and the gospel mission by consuming or hoarding what should be given.

I'm thankful that God has provided so that my children never go to bed hungry. I'm thankful for access to exceptional medical care. I'm thankful for our two cars and how they strengthen our ability to work, serve others, and fellowship in our suburban context. I'm also thankful for all those extras I've gotten to enjoy—delicious meals, good books, and memorable vacations. God is the creator of beauty and pleasure, and enjoying his gifts often stirs our hearts to delight in him, our glorious giver.

But in the midst of thanking God for his good gifts, it's tempting to believe we're at liberty to keep his provision to ourselves. Meanwhile there are people around the world going to bed hungry, being sold as slaves, and unreached by the gospel. We have brothers and sisters in Christ—whom God loves just as much as he loves us—enduring poverty and oppression. Instead of hoarding our Father's provision, will we be faithful to extend it to them?

It's a common trap to be thankful to God for prosperity while concurrently dishonoring him with it. John Piper challenges this inclination: "Gratitude for luxury impresses no one with our Savior. No matter how grateful we are, lining our lives with gold will not make the world think that our God is great. It will make the world think that our god is gold. That is no honor to the supremacy of his worth—none."[1]

### Hindrance #2: Materialism

We like to assume that we're not materialistic. I know I do. But the seduction of materialism is common to man, so we shouldn't assume we're above it. Ever so slowly, wants get shifted into categories of need, and we drift into embracing increasing levels of materialism. In order to be generous in the way Scripture instructs, we need to stop comparing ourselves to people who have more than we do and instead be molded by God's word.

If we find ourselves claiming ownership over our finances and prioritizing our interests over those revealed in Scripture, we'll inevitably miss out on the joy of generosity and rob ourselves of opportunities to practice contentment. Neglecting the poor in order to feed our material appetites breeds poverty in our own hearts. Cluttering our lives with the eternally meaningless makes us blind to the eternally meaningful. It's only our Savior, not our stuff, that will satisfy us.

We know real satisfaction is found in Christ, but we still seek satisfaction elsewhere. Scripture instructs, "If we have food and clothing, with these we will be content. But those who desire to

1    John Piper, "How Do You Synthesize Your Simple Lifestyle and Speaking at Expensive Conferences?," Desiring God, January 26, 2016, https://www.desiringgod.org/.

be rich fall into temptation, into a snare, into many senseless and harmful desires that plunge people into ruin and destruction" (1 Tim. 6:8–9). Yet we dismiss the danger of loving money and continually lengthen the list of things we think we need before we can be content. *If I have food and clothing, and a better house, and money for eating out, and an annual vacation, and updated electronics, and a decent retirement fund, and a cable subscription, and a new car—with these I will be content (maybe).* Our lists look different, of course, but we're all tempted to have them.

Usually our discontentment isn't very obvious, because most of us aren't buying luxury cars or expensive jewelry. We assume Jesus's command to not store up treasures on earth is just meant for those who have *more* treasures than we do. But he's speaking to all of us. The current of materialism is strong, and if we fail to fight against it, we'll tolerate it more and more. Our list of "needs" will just keep growing longer, and our list of excuses to neglect generosity will grow in proportion. All it takes is looking at our bank statements, bills, houses, closets, garages, sheds, and shelves to see that the vast majority of us don't have a problem with being too generous.

And though materialism is a common sin, its consequences are serious. It makes us ineffective witnesses as we embrace the same values the world embraces and strive for temporary comfort as if there's no such thing as heaven. It hurts people because the more we keep for ourselves, the less we can give to those in need. It ties our hearts to things of this earth, distracting us from the mission ahead of us and the kingdom awaiting us.

Randy Alcorn's teaching on money, possessions, and the glory of God has profoundly impacted my life. His idea of adopting a pilgrim mentality has been particularly useful in my battle against materialism:

> Pilgrims are unattached. They are travelers, not settlers, who are acutely aware that excessive things will distract and burden them. Material things are valuable to pilgrims, but only as they facilitate their mission. If you were traveling through a country on foot or on a bicycle, what would your attitude be toward possessions? You wouldn't hate them or think them evil—but you would choose them strategically. Unnecessary things would slow your journey or even force you to stop. . . . I'm convinced that the greatest deterrent to our giving is this: the illusion that earth, as it is now, is our home. Where we choose to store our treasures depends largely on where we think our home is. Those who think of earth as their real home will naturally want to pile up treasures here. Those who think of Heaven as their real home will naturally want to pile up treasures there. It all comes down to the question, "Where's your home?" To the Christian, God gives a clear answer. The only question is whether we'll live as if that answer is true.[2]

### Hindrance #3: Worldly Wisdom

Wisdom is a gift from God, and by all means, we should pursue it. But sometimes we mistake worldly wisdom for godly wisdom—especially in regard to money. Jesus illustrated this tendency in one of his parables, when he told the story of a man who appeared to be a wise steward (Luke 12:15–21). The guy worked

---

2  Randy Alcorn, "Having a Pilgrim Mentality about Money and Possessions," Eternal Perspectives Ministries, April 11, 2016, https://www.epm.org/.

hard, managed his property well, and produced an abundance of crops. He toiled and planned and saved so diligently that he had to build bigger barns just to store his harvest. Then he said to himself, "Soul, you have ample goods laid up for many years; relax, eat, drink, be merry" (12:19).

There's no indication that the man's wealth was accumulated through stealing or cheating or taking advantage of anyone, so it's a bit surprising when Jesus continues, "But God said to him, 'Fool! This night your soul is required of you, and the things you have prepared, whose will they be?' So is the one who lays up treasure for himself and is not rich toward God" (12:20–21). The man seemed to have it all together, but he was really a fool.

Some of us sin by being irresponsible with our money, but some of us sin precisely because we are so "responsible." We believe that wisdom is to think fifteen or fifty years ahead, but godly wisdom is to think fifty thousand years ahead. Instead of accumulating for ourselves, real wisdom stirs us to be rich toward God and sow to eternal investments. *All* our resources belong to God and are meant to fill his purposes, not our own desire for security and comfort. This doesn't mean we never save, but it reshapes our motives for doing so.

If we follow the example of this fool and consider it wisdom, it is likely that we have fallen into the trap of loving money. This trap is unsatisfying (Eccl. 5:10), foolish (Prov. 11:28), and dangerous (1 Tim. 6:10). It's easy to believe that the "love of money" only takes the face of Scrooge-like, miserly greed. But, like most sins, ungodly love for money is often subtle, socially acceptable, and easily entangling. We're not immune to its temptation!

*Hindrance #4: Anxiety*

The final common hindrance to generosity is anxiety. When our hope is in money to keep life stable or to improve our circumstances, we'll cling to control rather than opening our hands to others and entrusting ourselves to God. Jesus knows our propensity toward anxiety, so before delivering instructions about generosity, he preemptively offers this comfort:

> I tell you, do not be anxious about your life, what you will eat, nor about your body, what you will put on. For life is more than food, and the body more than clothing. Consider the ravens: they neither sow nor reap, they have neither storehouse nor barn, and yet God feeds them. Of how much more value are you than the birds! (Luke 12:22–24)

Jesus understands how trapped we become when we place our hope in possessions instead of in him. He wants us to be free. Our joy and peace will be completely unstable if they rest on things that will only pass away. When we're preoccupied with accumulating for our own security, we forfeit the opportunity to store up treasures in heaven that last forever.

It's hard not to trust in money, because money seems to offer deliverance from so many of our problems. But we can entrust ourselves to the God who feeds the ravens and clothes the lilies. How much more does he care about us? He will give us all we need—more than we need—because he gives us himself. We have a loving Father who delights to work for our good and his glory. There is nothing to fear and everything to look forward to when we forgo our wants and give to the needy. God graciously uses the act of giving to free us from the clutches of material anxiety so that we can trust him as our faithful provider.

## Fight Temptation

What are your weak spots? What are those areas in life that tempt you to be anxious, tightfisted, or materialistic? If you're unsure, ask God to show you. He will faithfully reveal your sin and patiently help you change. He *wants* you to experience the joy of giving.

Meditate on his word too. You're going to need it. Between our own sinful flesh and a culture that breeds covetousness, we're constantly fed the lie that we need more. The surest way to battle those lies is with the truth of Scripture. The sword of the Spirit—the word of God—arms us for this battle just like any other. It convicts and encourages and strengthens us. When we're tempted to hoard, Jesus reminds us, "Do not lay up for yourselves treasures on earth, where moth and rust destroy and where thieves break in and steal" (Matt. 6:19). When we're tempted to neglect generosity, Jesus reminds us, "Sell your possessions, and give to the needy. Provide yourselves with moneybags that do not grow old, with a treasure in the heavens that does not fail" (Luke 12:33). In the same way we use Scripture to battle against anger, lust, bitterness, anxiety, and pride, let us also use Scripture to battle against materialism, discontentment, greed, and lack of generosity. Without Scripture, we'll be weak in our fight against sin.

We also need accountability. While we tend to crave privacy and financial autonomy, Christian brothers and sisters are called to encourage, correct, and stir one another to follow Christ in *all* aspects of life. This includes our use of money. By living transparently among trusted friends, we're able to help one another honor God as faithful and generous stewards. The love of money is a dangerous trap, and one we shouldn't face alone. We need each other. This applies to married couples as well, and it helps to recognize that we might be tempted in different ways. I'm tempted to idolize financial security, while my husband, Andrew, is tempted to accumulate stuff he wants but doesn't need. He's helped me fight worry when money pressures arise, and I've helped him fight materialism and discontentment. All of us have different areas of strength and weakness, but God graciously enables us to stir each other to live generously.

## Biblical Examples of Generosity

Scripture tells of saints —both rich and poor—who were generous. We've already learned of Job's faithfulness and how he used his wealth for the good of the poor, the widow, and the orphan. His example shows that it's not inherently wrong to be rich, because riches sown righteously are pleasing to God. But it's a bit ironic that some of the most memorable examples of generosity didn't erupt from places of abundance but from people in need. Their examples challenge our own ungodly excuses and compel us to emulate cheerful giving. They also remind us that God weighs generosity by sacrifice, not sum—nothing goes beyond his notice.

### The Poor Widow

One day, Jesus was at the temple with his disciples. He'd been doing the usual—teaching, riling up the Pharisees, answering loaded questions—when he decided to sit and observe the temple treasury. As the bustling crowd threw heaps of money into the

THE MISSION OF MONEY

offering, the clanging of metals probably echoed through the temple. But then a poor widow approached and put in two small copper coins. Though they were only worth a penny, Jesus took notice. "And he called his disciples to him and said to them, 'Truly, I say to you, this poor widow has put in more than all those who are contributing to the offering box. For they all contributed out of their abundance, but she out of her poverty has put in everything she had, all she had to live on'" (Mark 12:43–44).

Talk about extravagant generosity! A desperately poor and vulnerable widow offered the Lord *everything* she had. Though we barely know anything about her, Jesus unveils two defining characteristics: the passion of her love and depth of her trust in God. Because God was her greatest treasure, she parted with her meager earthly treasure. And because she trusted God as her faithful provider, she entrusted herself to his care rather than seeking to control what little she had left. We can read this familiar story so quickly and give a quick nod to the poor widow's faith without ever thinking too deeply about her. There are only a few sentences referencing her in Scripture. But Jesus saw her. Jesus took note of her faith. He knew the overflowing love and trust reflected in those two small coins.

What she gave was nearly nothing, but Jesus declared it was *more* than the abundant offerings of the rich. His perspective should reassure us when we feel discouraged over the extent of needs to which we cannot contribute. We might desire to use our money for kingdom purposes but feel we have nothing good enough to offer. We might view our "small coins" as inconsequential. Yet when faith and love stir us to give generously from our circumstances, even what might be deemed meager gifts are considered more precious to God than the substantial gifts that represent the leftovers of abundance. When our congregation was raising money for a church building, offering baskets often included the contents of emptied piggy banks—pennies and dimes and one-dollar bills and even plastic gems. These gifts didn't make a dent in such monumental expenses, but nonetheless they were gifts that pleased the heart of God.

And let's not forget—God doesn't actually depend on us or our money. That's not the point of generosity. Just as he used two fish and five loaves to feed the five thousand, he can miraculously stretch a small contribution to accomplish mighty works.

### The Macedonian Church

We usually don't tell our congregations about another church's generosity, but Paul did. In his letter to the Corinthian church he wrote:

> We want you to know, brothers, about the grace of God that has been given among the churches of Macedonia, for in a severe test of affliction, their abundance of joy and their extreme poverty have overflowed in a wealth of generosity on their part. For they gave according to their means, as I can testify, and beyond their means, of their own accord, begging us earnestly for the favor of taking part in the relief of the saints—and this, not as we expected, but they gave themselves first to the Lord and then by the will of God to us. Accordingly, we urged Titus that as he had started, so he should complete among you this act of grace. But as you excel in everything—in faith, in speech,

in knowledge, in all earnestness, and in our love for you—see that you excel in this act of grace also. (2 Cor. 8:1–7)

The Macedonian church was suffering. We don't know all the details of their situation, but consider who was writing the letter. Paul had been beaten, stoned, shipwrecked, and imprisoned—I don't think he'd exaggerate and use terms like "severe affliction" lightly. The Macedonians' situation was so intense that he actually tried to resist their giving. But they ignored his pleas and gave out of an abundance of joy. Despite their poverty, generosity was the overflow of their hearts—so much so that they *begged* for the favor of giving. Rather than being absorbed in their own afflictions, they were filled with an earnest desire to use what they had—and more than they could afford—for the glory of God.

After celebrating the Macedonians' faithfulness, Paul urged the Corinthians to also excel in generosity—not out of compulsion but as a testament to their genuine love (2 Cor. 8:7–8). Christians give because they've received the generous grace of Jesus Christ. He was rich, but for our sake he emptied himself and became poor, so that we might enjoy the riches of forgiveness, relationship, and an inheritance with him (2 Cor. 8:9). Giving generously is one of the most profound ways we can emulate him.

### How to Cultivate Generosity

If we want to follow the examples of Job, the poor widow, and the Macedonian church, we must learn how to cultivate generosity. As we open our hands to God and our neighbor, his transforming grace will mold us into the cheerful givers he's created us to be.

*Give in Ways That Make No Earthly Sense*

Scripture sets the precedent that true generosity makes no earthly sense. It didn't make sense for the poor widow or the Macedonian church to give the way that they did, yet their examples illustrate the paradox that even when we're in need, we can overflow in generosity.

Proverbs instructs, "One gives freely, yet grows all the richer; another withholds what he should give, and only suffers want. Whoever brings blessing will be enriched, and one who waters will himself be watered" (11:24–25). The wisdom in this passage is so counterintuitive. As we freely give to others, God will care for us. As we seek to bless others, he will enrich our lives. But when we cling to our finances and possessions, we'll only end up with a greater sense of need. If we seek satisfaction where it can't be found, we'll just crave more stuff and more security. Giving freely refreshes our hearts and sharpens our vision to behold the blessings God has already provided.

Sometimes God's provision doesn't look like we'd expect. In the midst of saving for adoption, God led us to increase our monthly giving. As we obeyed, we were hit with various financial challenges. I lost my part-time job, and when I got a new one, it came with a significant pay cut. Then we had unforeseen expenses and bills due to healthcare costs and home repairs. It seemed that the more generously we sought to live, the more financial setbacks we faced. Yet God continually provided for all of our needs and worked to align our desires with his.

Sometimes his provision was miraculous. Right after I lost my job, friends gave us a substantial check toward our adoption. It would have been a blessing regardless of what had been going on, but at that particular time it was an especially encouraging display of God's faithfulness to meet our needs. By God's providence, Andrew had frequent opportunities to work overtime. We hadn't realized how much this added up until doing our taxes—we were blown away when we realized that all his extra work more than covered my decreased income. God provided later when friends, family, and our church generously supported us with adoption costs. Over the course of several months, our church's food ministry helped us save hundreds of dollars on groceries. And I'm confident there are countless expressions of provision we didn't even realize. Growing up, my parents often pointed out God's less obvious gifts—none of us needed orthodontic care, our old vans ran way longer than they should have. Everything that *doesn't* go wrong can be viewed as God's provision.

We'll all walk through seasons when there are sensible reasons to refrain from giving. But clinging to the promises of God as we seek to obey him is so much better than clinging to financial security. If we neglect to give in situations that require faith, we rob God of opportunities to prove himself more trustworthy than money.

Essentially, our lifestyles should be so generous that they make no sense to the world. If our spending habits appear responsible but our giving practices appear foolish, we're probably on the right track. Ultimately, whether poor or rich, the generosity of disciples should confound others and testify to the greater worth of Christ.

### Give Wisely

If we could only choose one passage to live by when it comes to money, it could be this: "Lay up for yourselves treasures in heaven, where neither moth nor rust destroys and where thieves do not break in and steal. For where your treasure is, there your heart will be also" (Matt. 6:20–21).

This passage conveys such simple instruction about how to direct our love. If we love God and want to love him more, we should give to his purposes. If we love our church and want to build the body of Christ and witness to our surrounding area, we should give to our church. If we know that Scripture commands us to care for the poor and oppressed but we lack a heart of love for them, *our hearts can be changed by giving*. God has given us a surefire way to cultivate love for his purposes and people—giving! Our hearts will follow our treasure. Randy Alcorn says it this way:

> Do you wish you cared more about eternal things? Then reallocate some of your money, maybe most of your money, from temporal things to eternal things. Put your resources, your assets, your money and possessions . . . into the things of God. Watch what happens. As surely as the compass needle follows north, your heart will follow your treasure. Money leads; hearts follow.[3]

When we give generously and strategically, God not only affects our hearts but furthers his mission. Through giving, Scripture can be translated, enabling people to read the riches of God's word in their native tongues. Through giving, churches can be planted and sustained all around the world to preach the good news, disciple believers, and witness to the lost. Through giving, water filtration

3   Randy Alcorn, "Where's Your Heart?," Eternal Perspectives Ministries, May 11, 2016, https://www.epm.org/.

systems can be installed, providing safe water for the rural poor. Through giving, starving children can be fed and naked children can be clothed. Through giving, urgent medical care can be provided, diseases can be treated, and surgical operations can be completed. Through giving, holistic healing can be offered to sexually trafficked women and children. Through giving, orphans can be provided for and adoptions can be funded. Through giving, education can be offered to the illiterate, and vocational training can be given to the outcast. There are endless and effective ways to give.

Many voices point to failures in charity as an excuse to refrain from giving. And, sadly, there are *many* examples of millions of dollars of aid being recklessly mismanaged and used in ways that have aggravated problems rather than helped them. But citing bad examples of charity or the uselessness of "throwing money at problems" doesn't diminish the Christian calling to give. Rather, it challenges us to thoughtfully and prayerfully discern how to steward our generosity. (I've included a resource to help you think through this in the appendix.)

There are destitute people spanning the globe whom we can richly bless if we share our wealth and live with less. Sometimes we get to extend this care personally through relationships with people facing need. We can also invest in worthy organizations and ministries, helping them sustain and expand their programs. If we're willing to invest time identifying efforts that employ wise practices and are managed with financial integrity, we'll find effective avenues to direct our support.

Because needs are endless and money isn't, I find it helpful to consider prioritizing three basic categories addressed in Scripture. Before spending money on optional items (e.g., vacation, extra clothes, gym memberships, cable/Netflix, eating out, home décor), are we prioritizing the needs of our local church, our brothers and sisters in Christ, and at least one suffering people group? We can weigh our individual opportunities based on proximity, relationship, and awareness and then give as God leads through the means he's provided. But regularly implementing planned giving and responding to the Holy Spirit's unexpected promptings keeps generosity a priority in our hearts.

## Joyfully Anticipate the Reward

When we truly trust God's character, we find the confidence to live generously (Mal. 3:6–10). If God's love is so great that he sacrificed his Son to buy our redemption, would he cheat us by withholding anything good? No. He will richly reward us. We serve the same Father who spoke through Isaiah:

> If you pour yourself out for the hungry
>     and satisfy the desire of the afflicted,
> then shall your light rise in the darkness
>     and your gloom be as the noonday.
> And the LORD will guide you continually
>     and satisfy your desire in scorched places
>     and make your bones strong;
> and you shall be like a watered garden,
>     like a spring of water,
>         whose waters do not fail. (Isa. 58:10–11)

Jesus taught, "It is more blessed to give than to receive" (Acts 20.35). This simple message is easy to forget, or worse, to distrust. But if Jesus says it is more blessed to give than to receive, it truly is. He knows that any possessions or experiences we buy won't satisfy us. It all comes up short. But he never comes up short. By loosening our grasp on money and possessions, our hands are freed to take hold of him. When we set our eyes on our eternal home instead of our earthly one, we'll stop storing up treasures that'll only be destroyed. When we trust his generous character and the promise of reward, what we sacrifice here won't end up seeming so sacrificial. Jesus doesn't teach self-denial for the sake of self-denial. He doesn't preach a gospel of minimalism and simplicity—he's a God of abundance! When he calls us to die to ourselves, it's so we can know his exceeding worth. When Christ is our treasure, we'll never regret any act of generosity.

"The point is this: whoever sows sparingly will also reap sparingly, and whoever sows bountifully will also reap bountifully. . . . God loves a cheerful giver" (2 Cor. 9:6–7). Not only does God love a cheerful giver, but he's the one who makes a cheerful giver. The more we give, the more joy we find in doing so. The more we give, the more we discover that giving is a privilege that surpasses the fleeting pleasures of wealth and security. Giving generously reaps happiness.

And someday, God will extravagantly reward our obedience. No matter how small or private, no act of generosity done for his glory goes unnoticed. You might cringe at the thought of being motivated by reward. It doesn't sound very godly. But would God tell us about the rewards awaiting us if it was sinful to be motivated by them? He's the one who wired us to be motivated by both love and reward—the two don't act in opposition to each other. We can give out of love for God *and* eager anticipation of his rewards. Isn't that exciting?

We might give up our dream homes here, but if it means we get to have the great architect create infinitely better homes in his kingdom, it's worth it. Any earthly passion we sacrifice in worship will be rewarded with something greater. I love to travel, but maybe I'll never go anywhere noteworthy again. I don't know what the future holds. But if that's the case, there's absolutely no reason for me to feel like I'm missing out, because in heaven I'll get to explore beautiful places beyond my imagination. I'll eat food more delicious than what I ate in Italy. I'll marvel at mountains more beautiful than those I hiked in Switzerland. I'll traverse cities more fascinating than Rome (and there'll be no pollution or garbage to disturb their beauty). I'll see colors more vibrant than those in India, and rather than seeing hungry children begging on the streets, I'll see fellow saints joyfully worshiping God. Everything here is only a shadow of the beauty to come. Any sacrifices we make on earth to serve the Lord and love others will be abundantly rewarded in heaven. He won't let us outgive him. "Any temporal possession can be turned into everlasting wealth. Whatever is given to Christ is immediately touched with immortality."[4]

## Discussion Questions

1. Consider the common temptations we face in regard to money. What usually hinders you from living generously? What Bible verses can you meditate on to fight those temptations?

4   A. W. Tozer, in Randy Alcorn, "Eleven of Randy Alcorn's Favorite Quotes," Eternal Perspectives Ministries, January 12, 2010, https://www.epm.org/.

2. Read Matthew 6:20–21. Consider where you've been storing your treasure. What does that reflect about your heart?

3. How has giving generously brought you joy in the past? How can you grow as a cheerful giver now?

4. Consider needs among people in your church or your community. How can you extend generosity to meet those needs?

5. Jesus instructs that our giving should be in secret (see Matt. 6:1–4), but he also drew attention to the generosity of the poor widow, and Paul publicly shared about the generosity of the Macedonian church. What is at the heart of the instruction to give in secret? What should be our motivation when we *do* discuss money/giving among other Christians?

# 7

# Our Homes Are a Base for Mercy

I LOVE A GOOD home renovation show. *Love It or List It*, *Property Brothers*, and, of course, *Fixer Upper* are among my favorites. There's something so satisfying about seeing a dated or derelict house transformed into something beautiful. Created by a God who designed a beautiful world, we're naturally drawn to warm and creative spaces. But like so many God-given instincts, our desires are often warped by sin and driven by selfishness. This includes how we think about our homes. Our homes aren't only meant to meet our needs but to serve God's mission. Our living spaces should be places of ministry. So there are multiple things to consider even before we rent, buy, upsize, or downsize —considerations that should be rooted in a desire to honor God. And since he's commanded us to love our neighbors as ourselves, our housing choices should reflect that we're not only looking to our own interests but also to the interests of others.

Before laying down roots—or uprooting and going elsewhere— we need to consider *where* God might call us. For those who've grown up in middle- and upper-class communities, it's easy to assume that we should always live in areas with good school systems, safe neighborhoods, and nice houses. There certainly isn't anything intrinsically wrong with these locations, but perhaps this "automatic" mindset has caused many of us to miss opportunities elsewhere.

I confess to having this assumption when my husband and I were looking for our first house. There were multiple towns that we considered out of the question without any prayerful consideration. We felt entitled to "nice and safe," because that's how we grew up—we didn't even engage the Lord about it. But God desires to pervade every place with his people for his good purposes. So he might call some of us—even if we're used to comfortable suburbs, or have young kids, or can afford nice houses—to joyfully live in areas that lack those qualities, places that might even be considered unsafe.

A single woman moved to South Philadelphia for a church plant and lived on what was considered a "shady" street. While living there, she sought to be a light by frequently welcoming underprivileged children into her home who would have otherwise been alone after school. Because of her willingness to move where others might avoid and to engage where others might ignore, numerous children were exposed to the love of Christ as it emanated from her home. Oh, if more of us would follow her example! Instead of closing our doors and building high fences, let us open our doors and let our light shine forth into the darkness.

Wherever we choose to live, we have far more important questions to consider than whether there's enough closet space. We must consider whether our choices will help or hinder our ability to live generously, to welcome others, to be committed to our churches, and to be servants in our communities.

## Think Globally, Act Locally

As Christians we should always be thinking globally because the entire world is in need of the gospel and renewal. But God puts us in specific locations for specific purposes. So our primary call to be doers of mercy isn't in faraway countries—it's right where we live. Extending mercy through prayer, generosity, and advocacy certainly can stretch to those we'll never meet, but God's *primary* method of advancing his redemptive work is through relationships. When Jesus instructed his followers to go and make disciples of all nations and to bring salvation to the ends of the earth, we are among the recipients. The good news secured at Golgotha made its way across countries and oceans to reach *this* nation, and disciples residing here are called to participate in its continued spread. When we demonstrate mercy and provide practical care to unbelievers within relational contexts, our evangelistic message to them is amplified. When we care for the needs of our brothers and sisters in Christ in a local-church context, the testimony of the church is a witness to the watching world.

God has placed us in our families, neighborhoods, workplaces, cities, and states to reach people. Rich or poor, every soul matters to Christ. His saving grace is offered to the malnourished widow in Ethiopia and the successful lawyer in Manhattan. It's offered to the child laborer, and to the Ivy League student. It's needed in successful suburban communities and struggling rural communities. It's needed among the urban elite and the urban poor. While physical needs vary greatly, all of humanity shares the desperate need to be reconciled with God. Knowing this compels the urgency of our mission wherever we reside.

It's easier for me to feel compassion for the poor than for the middle class. I can long to be in the slums of India laboring for Christ rather than in my own neighborhood. I can romanticize what life and ministry would be like and conjure a story that casts me as a steadfast servant and passionate witness. I forget that all my sinful tendencies will follow me wherever I go. I also struggle to have compassion toward those in my area because of self-righteousness and pride. I'm tempted to feel that the poor "deserve" the gospel, while if the rich pass it up, well, they had their chance. The truth is, none of us deserves the gospel. Apart from Christ, all of us deserve God's wrath instead of his love. All of us deserve to be cast away from him rather than brought into his family. And when I lack compassion for my neighbors simply because they have material goods, I need to repent.

In the same way we're not reflecting the love and grace of Christ when we neglect the physical needs of the poor, we're not reflecting the love and grace of Christ when we neglect the spiritual needs of the rich. The same Savior who reached out to prostitutes reached out to tax collectors. The same Savior who welcomed little children intervened in the life of a Pharisee. If we elevate reaching the poor and oppressed *at the neglect* of the rich and powerful, we're failing to emulate the impartial compassion of Christ. I can't shut my eyes to my actual neighbors and then pat myself on the back because I care for people halfway around the world. To do so would be shortsighted, revealing that I am more aware of earthly trials than eternal trajectories. My neighbors next door might not be suffering greatly in a material sense, but I can't view them apathetically when their eternity is at stake.

Furthermore, God desires to use us as extensions of his merciful provision and care *even* when the needs of those we encounter don't seem desperate. I've often failed miserably at this. I love being generous to those I deem "truly in need" but am tight-fisted toward those facing moderate struggles. I'm eager to serve those whose situations are obviously dire and can grumble to serve those in less difficult circumstances. The Puritan preacher Jonathan Edwards said that such a mindset is contrary to the rule of loving our neighbors as ourselves: "Love towards our neighbor should work in the same manner, and express itself in the same ways, as our love for ourselves. . . . We should in like manner lay out ourselves to obtain relief for [our neighbor], though his difficulties be not extreme."[1] Just as I hope others would come to my aid *before* I reached a point of desperation, I shouldn't overlook the less urgent needs of others.

If we want our reach to go past where we are, we need to start where we are. We must be vigilant to pray for opportunities as we go about our daily lives, recognizing that we are constantly surrounded by people in need of God. All of us are called to demonstrate his mercy and live for his mission in whatever spheres we live our lives, starting in our homes and extending into our communities.

## Hospitality

Can I let you in on an embarrassing secret? When I hear someone at the door, my instinct is to breathe a frustrated sigh as numerous

1   Jonathan Edwards, cited in Timothy Keller, *Ministries of Mercy: The Call of the Jericho Road* (Phillipsburg, NJ: P&R, 1997), 99.

thoughts race through my head. *I don't feel like inviting anyone in. I have so many things to do! Oh, no, my house is a mess. I don't even recognize this person. What could he possibly want? Maybe I'll just pretend I'm not home.* Relief sweeps over me when I open the door and see the person holding a package. Only a delivery guy! I smile broadly, thank him, and sign the receipt. Later on, Andrew suggests that we invite our neighbors over. Incredulous, I resist. I enjoy their company, but we *just* had them over. He raises an eyebrow and reminds me that that was actually six months ago; it's probably about time to invite them for dinner again.

Even in regard to the people I love most, I struggle to proactively pursue hospitality. When people drop by unannounced, the vibes I give probably make them feel like an intrusion rather than a welcome interruption. My home feels like *my* domain. I want to control when and where I pursue others. I want people over only when my house looks nice, and I don't want the burden of cleaning when it's a mess.

Clearly, when it comes to lessons in hospitality, I am the example of what not to be. Given that it's such a weakness of mine, I spent years undermining the spiritual significance of hospitality. It was nothing more than a box to check off, and I met my "quota" by hosting a church small group twice a month. But as I studied Scripture, God convicted me. Not only was I called to grow in this practice for the mere purpose of obedience (Heb. 13:2; 1 Pet. 4:9), but I began to realize how much hospitality and mercy go hand in hand.

If our mercy is meant to reflect the God we love, we must strive to emulate the ways in which he's shown us mercy. And God is hospitable! His hospitality dates back to Genesis 1. He created a beautiful and bountiful world for us to live in—a home that abundantly provided for every need. When Adam and Eve disobeyed and sin entered the earth, this home was broken, leading to God's second great act of hospitality. In mercy, Jesus humbled himself by coming to share a home with us; the Creator of heaven and earth stepped down from his throne to dwell among lowly men. Because he lived among us in perfect righteousness, his death secured our access to enjoy an eternal home with him. Those who were strangers and enemies now have an open invitation to dwell in his kingdom. He is preparing a feast, a city, a new heavens and a new earth—a new *home*—where he will welcome us for eternity. Why? Because he is a mercifully hospitable God.

When we open our lives in hospitality, reaching out in ways that comfort the lonely, provide for the afflicted, and turn strangers into friends, we're imaging Christ. When we don't just serve people from a distance but go a step further to invite them into our lives, we're imitating our hospitable God who in humility came to us and in grace will bring us back with him.

Imitating the hospitality of God means more than throwing dinner parties for our friends and family. Although biblical hospitality *includes* fellowship among believers, it's *also* meant to be evangelistic and service oriented in nature. It should welcome strangers and reach into our communities. All of us have unbelieving neighbors, and opening our homes paves the way for interactions that go deeper than driveway small talk. In a world that's increasingly individualistic, the act of inviting others to dine at our tables, make messes of our houses, and relax on our couches offers the comfort of community and creates an environment to show mercy. Our neighbors struggle in ways we don't know.

Even if everything appears fine on the outside, there may be ways they're suffering because of sickness, loneliness, loss, addiction, or abuse. But we'll never know the struggles they face if we fail to welcome them into our lives. And if we don't know, how can we show them mercy? To love our neighbors as Jesus loves us, we must actually get to know them.

We must also hospitably welcome those whom society overlooks or deems unlovely. Jesus says in Luke, "When you give a dinner or a banquet, do not invite your friends or your brothers or your relatives or rich neighbors, lest they also invite you in return and you be repaid. But when you give a feast, invite the poor, the crippled, the lame, the blind, and you will be blessed, because they cannot repay you" (Luke 14:12–14). When we reach out to those whom others disregard, we're reflecting the heart of God. He seeks the outcast. The forgotten. The shoved aside. The socially awkward. The dismissed. The disparaged. The despised. He shows no partiality and isn't impressed by status, appearance, or charisma. Rather, he sees and cares for the lonely and left out. Will we do the same?

If you're anything like me, you probably find it intimidating to reach out to people you barely know. We worry that it'll be uncomfortable—and it might be! But Scripture instructs us to show hospitality to strangers (Heb. 13:2) and soberly warns that neglecting to do so is the equivalent of being unwelcoming to Christ (Matt. 25:44–45). Knowing this means I can't hide behind my long-held excuse that "hospitality isn't my gifting"; rather, it pushes me to desperately depend on Christ as I seek to grow in a very unnatural grace. And he has helped me. Even though I still wrestle with weaknesses and sin, he is faithfully transforming me. By his grace, I have grown in hospitality. Now, instead of dreading the knock on the door, I've begun to look forward to it. Just yesterday a neighborhood kid knocked and asked if he could use our new basketball hoop, and I told him we're happy to let him use it whenever he wants. It's just a little thing, but hopefully, over time, this kid will know that our house is a place where he's welcome.

While God calls and enables all believers to practice hospitality, it's helpful to remember that the particulars *don't* need to look the same—he's gifted us in different ways. My mother-in-law shows hospitality by inviting and feeding people by the dozens. If you have nowhere to go for the holiday, you will get an invitation to her home. My sister shows hospitality by hosting neighborhood playdates, spontaneously babysitting for friends, and inviting neighbors in for coffee. Lee will cook you a stellar meal, Robin will invite you to use her pool, and Hannah will let you stay late into the night (I, on the other hand, couldn't resist buying a welcome mat that says: "Be our guest! Please leave by 9"). Whether your strength lies in a high capacity to welcome many, show spontaneous service, share home-cooked meals, or you're like me and consider it a huge win when you remember to offer your guest a glass of water, we can all strive to bless others with a welcoming home.

On a larger scale, there are unique long-term opportunities to show hospitality. Some of you will open your homes to exchange students or aging parents. Some of you will welcome children in foster care or adults recovering from addiction. I know a family of seven who welcomed a family of five to live with them for a year in their modest Cape Cod–style home after they'd become homeless. Whether we welcome the sad or the sick, the solitary or the stranger, there are all sorts of ways to use our homes as places of comfort and ministry to others.

Nobody has exemplified a heart of hospitality to me more than my grandparents. I honestly can't remember a time when they didn't have someone living with them. Over the course of decades they've welcomed troubled teens, homeless women, single women, families in need, and families in transition to live with them for extended periods of time. Even when they were almost sixty— a season when so many people start to wind down and dream of retirement and relaxation—they had my grandmother's aging parents come live with them until their passing almost *ten* years later. Their bighearted hospitality has been a powerful expression of God's welcoming mercy.

## Orienting the Household

Building Christ-centered households means reorienting everyday life. If this book has convinced you that extending mercy to the needy is a primary way of imaging Christ, it's important to orient your household with this in mind. Whether we live with roommates, on our own (and in fellowship with others), or with our families, we can encourage one another to use our words, our influence, and our resources to care for those in need. We can stir one another to be doers of mercy in the day-to-day.

### Mercy-Oriented Marriage

God ordained the institution of marriage to depict the covenant love between Christ and his bride, the church. When marriage functions as God designed, it points us to joyfully anticipate our eternal union with Christ. The love and faithfulness expressed in the context of marriage is just a foretaste of a better one, when a chorus of thundering voices will exclaim:

Hallelujah!
For the Lord our God
   the Almighty reigns.
Let us rejoice and exult
   and give him the glory,
for the marriage of the Lamb has come,
   and his Bride has made herself ready. (Rev. 19:6–7)

Marriage isn't ultimately about a husband and a wife; it's about the glory of God. As such, it's designed to refine us, to make us holy as he is holy. If Christians are called to stir up one another toward love and good works, how much more should a husband and wife be devoted to each other's sanctification! Building Christ-centered marriages means helping each other walk in obedience in all things, which necessitates prioritizing God's mercy-filled mission in everyday life. As our love for God and each other grows, it will naturally overflow toward others. Remembering how Christ has loved and served us, we'll encourage each other to love and serve those in need.

Since service outside the home often involves sacrifice in the home, it's important for husbands and wives to release and encourage each other. Andrew has always excelled at this. He's taken time off work to watch the kids so that I could bring a Syrian friend to the hospital for a C-section. He's encouraged me to press on when I've felt weary and helped me discern when I've taken on more than I could (or should) handle. While he's always joyfully released me to serve others, I've struggled to reciprocate. He spent a few years mentoring teens through a local nonprofit. In theory, I was fully supportive. How could I not be on board with his desire to invest time as a positive male role model and an evangelistic witness in a kid's life? But in reality it was a different story. When we'd already had a busy week and I just wanted an evening home together, I was tempted to resent him spending his time elsewhere. When the kid he mentored came over on weekends, I struggled not to view him as an infringement on our family time. Honestly, it's just easier to find joy doing "good works" myself than releasing Andrew to do them. But if my service is really to be selfless, I can't monopolize our mercy endeavors and must encourage Andrew's devotion to do the same. For most couples, living as demonstrators of mercy requires this type of partnership. Some efforts can be done together, but some require one spouse to take on the unseen and humble role of supporting the doer. It may be less glamorous, but it's no less important.

It's also vital to walk in unity. If, in our attempts to "go and do likewise," we end up dishonoring our spouse, we're missing the big picture of glorifying God. Since our marriages are to be a picture of Christ and his church, we must never sacrifice devotion to our spouse in the name of mercy or mission. Sometimes these tensions erupt over big decisions, like when one spouse wants to adopt and the other doesn't. More commonly, disunity is provoked by small and everyday disagreements. Once I got into an argument with Andrew over something he'd been spending money on because I thought it'd be better to give the money away. During this argument I was angry and self-righteous and demeaning in the way that I spoke to him. The godly desire to live generously had morphed into an idol, exposed in my willingness to sin against my husband to pursue it. It was no longer about the glory of God. We need to be ready for these kinds of tensions and temptations.

In situations where a husband and wife aren't in unity—particularly if one spouse isn't a believer—we need to prioritize expressing our covenant love to *our spouse*. As we're faithful in that, God will show us ways we can still pursue mercy toward others. Even when our circumstances are limiting, God intimately knows our hearts and is pleased by what might feel like "hindered" obedience. If husbands and wives can't give as generously, serve as frequently, or show hospitality as often as they'd like for the sake of honoring their spouse, God sees the little choices they make to be faithful where they can. Being consistent doers of mercy is certainly easier to pursue when both husband and wife are committed (and it might produce more visible fruit), but God is just as glorified by those who seek to honor him despite the trial of being unsupported in such endeavors.

### *Parenting: Part of the Mission, for the Mission*

Parenting is a profound way to train future colaborers in Christ. As we pray for the Holy Spirit to liven children's hearts to saving faith, we get to teach and exemplify what it means to live out that faith. Like us, our children are naturally selfish. They'll desire a comfortable gospel, craving the picture of a God who offers the gift of everything and commands the sacrifice of nothing. But that's not how the gospel works. Grace alone secures our salvation, but saving grace has transformative implications. For our children to know the happiness and satisfaction that's found only in Christ, they must learn to take up their cross daily to follow him (see Luke 9:23). For our children to live in the reality that their life is not their own (1 Cor. 6:19–20), they must realize that they were bought with a price and that all the gifts they enjoy have been given by God as tools to serve him and love others.

When it comes to parenting—and probably mothering in particular—there are two mindsets we're tempted to adopt that undermine this work of raising colaborers in Christ. Some of us lack vision for the high call of raising children. We're tempted to see them as distractions from the truly important work, and the labor of parenting stirs discontentment because it restricts time we think could be better spent elsewhere. But moms and dads, be encouraged—faithful parenting is one of the most powerful opportunities we will *ever* have to make disciples of Jesus, to help form people who "go and do likewise." As parents, we're given daily opportunities to magnify the depth of Christ's love and the beauty of his grace. As we joyfully obey and follow Christ, our lives testify to our children of his unmatchable worth. Rather than resenting or undermining our roles as parents, we should be enthralled with the privilege and responsibility of raising our children in the knowledge of the Lord.

The other common mindset is found among those who embrace the importance of loving their children but swing too strongly on the other side of the pendulum. Family becomes all-encompassing, leaving no room for service outside the home. We want to guard our children from discomfort and sacrifice—to protect them from the cost of following Christ. An initially godly effort to be faithful parents can inadvertently diminish other biblical priorities. If we're teaching our children about loving Christ, we can't fail to point them to the *outward* purposes that personal relationships with Jesus entail. Our mission starts in the home—*but it doesn't end there.*

Ultimately, to be doers of mercy our lives must be centered on our Father, not our children. We exist to serve him, to make his name known, and to reflect his character to others. Of course, the daily laying down of our lives to nurture, serve, and enjoy our children is an expression of God's love. But sometimes the lines are blurred, and we lose the part where it's about God and his glory and make it too much about our children and their desires. If our lives are so centered on our kids that they don't witness us serving and extending mercy to *others*, we're missing an important piece of discipleship.

Because of this tendency to swing too far on one side of the pendulum to the other, it's often difficult to discern how to glorify God *in* our roles without being controlled *by* our roles. We continually have to evaluate questions that don't necessarily have right or wrong answers. *Should I stretch myself to serve others more or do I need to reprioritize time at home because I've been overextended? Should I accompany my friend to her doctor's appointment and miss my son's soccer game? Should I give this bonus to the poor, or save it for my child's college tuition?* Because so many of these questions lack definitive answers, we must keep seeking wisdom from the Lord, knowing that he gives it generously to all who ask (James 1:5). When we diligently pursue wisdom through prayer, studying Scripture, and seeking godly counsel from others, God will lead us through our changing seasons and situations.

When evaluating competing goods, it's helpful to have a sense of triage. How are your kids doing? How will this choice or sacrifice affect them? Are you being faithful to tend to their struggles and spiritual health first? How urgent is the outside need? Wess Stafford, former president of Compassion International, is a great example. His work and its travel demands involved plenty of sacrifice for his family, but he still recognized that ministry to orphaned children didn't usurp his *higher* call of fatherhood. He wrote:

> When all is said and done and I stand before my Lord, I am sure he will value more what I have done in faithfulness to my two children than the ministry to millions of children in poverty. I don't know what you are doing in the workplace or what impact on the world you are making, but if you have children entrusted to you, I am dead certain the same is for you. They are precious, deserving of our time, attention, and serious commitment.[2]

A beautiful way to marry the priorities of caring for our children and caring for the needy is to do ministry with our kids. It's an example to our children when they see us taking time on a Saturday to cook a meal for a sick neighbor, but it's even better if they help us make it. It's an example to our children when we have a weekly commitment to serve the homeless, but it's even better if we bring them along. It's an example to our children when they see us sacrificing personal desires in order to give generously to others, but it's even better if we brainstorm and make giving goals together.

During my kids' little years, it took trial and error to discern what types of service were worthwhile with them in tow. One time

2   Wess Stafford, *Too Small to Ignore: Why the Least of These Matters Most* (Colorado Springs, CO: WaterBrook Press, 2007), 34.

I volunteered to help at a holiday party for refugees, and it was a total disaster. It was crowded and chaotic, and my children were so overwhelmed and stressed that all my attention was focused on them, hindering me from actually helping with the event. We had to find a different setting to serve. When I discussed this burden with one of the social workers, God orchestrated the perfect opportunity. She told me of a relocated family who was isolated from the rest of their local refugee community because they had no driver's license or car. The mother needed an English tutor and help with transportation—something I could provide. Her youngest son needed socialization because he was too young to attend school—something my kids could provide. For six months (until they ended up moving out of state), we visited once a week. I helped her with English lessons, we ran errands, and our kids played together. There were still plenty of challenges to work through—communication barriers and cultural differences, and our two-year-olds may or may not have gotten into a full-blown fistfight at the DMV—but it was a much better fit than attempting to help at a big event. My kids played a genuine role in serving, and our families built a close relationship that continues today.

Including our kids in service is especially important in the teenage years. Mary, a woman I met at a conference, told me of her involvement with an organization working to eradicate sex trafficking and minister to those in the sex industry in her state. It was particularly compelling to hear how she included her teenaged son. She wanted him to see the dark side of the porn industry—how it grieves God and preys on women. She wanted him to grow compassion for those trapped in prostitution and to become a man who values and protects women. Many parents try to shield their children from this type of darkness in the world, but Mary gave her son the opportunity to interact with the grave evil of sin and witness the redemptive work of the Savior.

We all have different capacities, limitations, financial situations, and family dynamics, so life's details are going to look different (and probably change from season to season). But as Christians, there are biblical principles that are true for all of us. Mothers and fathers aren't exempt from scriptural commands to care for the poor and seek justice for the oppressed. We aren't exempt from taking risks and making sacrifices for the good of those *outside* our families. We must not mistake worshiping God through parenting with worshiping parenting itself. When we do, the good gift of family becomes an idol that causes us to neglect the obedience that occurs outside the home. We must remember that our primary identity is not in being parents but in being sons and daughters of the Father.

## Community Outreach

In America there might not be widespread famine or sprawling slums, yet it's important to remember that the poor are here. There are American children going to bed without dinner. There are women here suffering physical and sexual abuse from men. There are men here being discriminated against because of the color of their skin or the language they speak. There are families here who have fled the terrors of war and persecution. There are people here who are marginalized and mistreated because of their mental or physical disabilities. There is loss, there is heartbreak, there is darkness *here*.

To some, I'm stating the obvious. Some of you live in places where needs aren't only apparent, but overwhelming. Your struggle to help isn't related to a lack of awareness or opportunity— rather, you need wisdom about how to steward your limited time and resources in a vast sea of suffering. But those in middle- to upper-class contexts have difficulty identifying these hardships. Christians in these contexts have to be intentional to identify local needs and then proactively seek ways to respond and serve in our communities as doers of mercy.

Michael and Mandy lived in California, surrounded by plenty of prosperity. In the midst of working, graduate school, and life as newlyweds, they also wanted to identify and serve needs in their community. This led Michael to volunteer as a tutor to immigrant students—kids whose parents worked long hours and often couldn't help with schoolwork due to language barriers. Later, Mandy jumped in, and God used their presence as a couple to establish a deeper friendship with the boys.

Even though it was a new and busy season of their lives—a time when it would've been easy to justify withdrawing from outreach—Michael and Mandy pressed in more, eventually moving into a mentoring role with the boys. Every Friday night they'd hang out—which is pretty remarkable, when you think of the many ways a group of teenagers and a busy couple could spend their Friday nights. They loved to be together, so they'd play games, watch movies, discuss life, and plan for the future. The boys shared their fears and aspirations, their trials and passions. Because of cultivating such a deep and mutual love, Michael and Mandy not only served practical needs but invested spiritually and demonstrated the love of Christ.

If we—like Michael and Mandy—intentionally *seek* opportunities to demonstrate mercy, we'll find them. In some places, there's a high concentration of homelessness, fatherlessness, and addiction. In others, the greatest need might be among the elderly or the disabled. More often than not, there are many different types of people struggling and suffering and many different ways to respond.

Even though I live in a safe neighborhood, I'm only about thirty minutes from one of the most dangerous places in the country. Drugs, violence, and prostitution are prevalent, and children too frequently suffer in broken and unstable homes. Even closer to my house are refugees struggling to make a new life after escaping persecution and war-ravaged countries. There's a nearby nursing home where physical needs are met but hearts are lonely. My small state has a high concentration of children with autism, as well as one of the highest rates of abortion. On top of all this, there are children in foster care throughout my county. It doesn't take long to realize that despite living in a comfortable suburb, there are actually *many* opportunities to serve the vulnerable nearby.

A few women in my church are heavily involved with outreach to local prostitutes. They are doing amazing work in a dark and discouraging domain. They see more relapse than they do redemption, but they press on because they hope in the God who seeks and saves the lost. The ministry leader, Brenda, treats these women like treasured daughters—stroking their unwashed hair, rubbing their syringe-scarred arms, embracing their used and abused bodies. She pours out her heart and her life for them, demonstrating the love of the Savior who doesn't just rehabilitate but has the power to redeem.

We should be encouraged by these types of examples without feeling weighed down by the notion that we must imitate the outworking of someone else's faith. God's word is true for every Christian, but he designed the church to be diverse in gifting, passion, and resources for a reason. We're not all Michaels or Mandys, but we all can emulate their service. We're not all Brendas, but we all can emulate her love. We're not all sent to the same people, but we're all sent somewhere. The question is, who does God want us to serve?

I've shared a lot about my involvement with local refugees, but I think it's important for you to know what a rocky start it was. When the unforgettable photograph of three-year-old Alan Kurdi's dead body on a European shore gripped the world, God first gripped my heart. I started paying attention to news reports and statistics, finding the refugee crisis to be far greater than I ever imagined. The more I prayed and sought to respond in generosity, the more emotionally invested I became. With increasing clarity, the Spirit impressed on me a desire to serve and build friendships within the Muslim refugee community. The problem was that I didn't know how! It seemed like every organization I sought out either didn't work locally or had only full-time career positions. After *months* of frustration, I finally found an avenue to volunteer—a place that could connect me with the refugees I wanted to serve but didn't know how to find. This is an example of why we shouldn't passively adopt the mindset of "Wait for God to open a door" or "Let go and let God." Jesus doesn't take the wheel and drive us through serene and open roads while we close our eyes and await our destination. He teaches us to navigate roadblocks, work through confusion, and overcome challenges in order to obey. He leads us *and* enables us to take responsibility.

There are many other ways I *could* serve in my community, but opportunity isn't the same as calling. I'm finite. So are you. I can't do everything. Neither can you. This is why we must remember the importance of the local church. Though we have our own limitations, we can stir up one another to love and good works. As we serve in specific ways and encourage our Christian brothers and sisters who serve elsewhere, we collectively show our communities the mercy of our King.

## When Mercy Leads to Relationship

God is a God of relationship. He doesn't just do things *for* us, he seeks relationship *with* us. He lived *among* us. He walked with Adam and Eve in the garden. When sin ruined that communion, he still manifested his presence to his people. He led the Israelites through the wilderness in a pillar of cloud and a pillar of fire. His presence filled the temple. And then he came— as God incarnate—into the world. He humbled himself and became man *to be with us*. And after his ascension, at Pentecost, he gave us the gift of his Spirit. In Christ, we are never alone. God could've just saved us from his wrath. Instead, he desires relationship. Someday we will experience the fullness of his presence again—his dwelling place will be with us (Rev. 21:3).

As imitators of God, our expressions of mercy should lead us into relationships. Rather than being content to just do things for others, we'll long to build relationships with others. Of course, this isn't always possible, and we can joyfully help and minister to those we'll never see again. We can generously support ministries serving people we'll never even meet. But serving in our own communities gives us the opportunity to build actual and lasting relationships.

I started serving refugees as a volunteer. I filled out paperwork and did background checks and met with social workers—the whole deal. But I don't consider myself a volunteer anymore. Now these families are just my friends. We celebrate birthdays, go to the park together, and text each other. Though I still seek to serve them, there's a reciprocity to the relationship. I help them fill out forms for school, but they make me dinner. And the deeper our relationship grows, the more we're able to demonstrate the love of God and point them to their need for relationship with him.

Though volunteering is a great way to get connected with needs in your area, it's not always necessary either. Growing up, my parents always had our doors open to people in the neighborhood. Almost every day we could expect a knock around the time school got out. Some kids had challenging family dynamics, and what drew them to visit our house wasn't just to play with friends but to be around loving adults—they saw the gospel through my parents. Their warm relationship had an effect.

Are we being faithful witnesses in the contexts God has placed us? Are we aware of the needs facing those in our communities and looking for ways to meet them? Are we intentional about building real relationships with unbelievers? God sacrificed his own Son to build a relationship with us. What will we sacrifice to build relationships with our neighbors?

**Discussion Questions**

1. Is hospitality a priority for you? Why or why not?

2. Read Luke 14:12–14. How can you grow in showing hospitality to people who might be overlooked?

3. Describe the observable demographics of where you live. What needs are most apparent among your neighbors and community? How might God be calling you to respond?

4. In what ways have you oriented your household to serve those in need? In what ways should you make adjustments?

5. How are you seeking to build genuine relationships with the people you serve?

8

# Where Do We Go from Here?

WHEN I READ BOOKS on Christian growth and living, I regularly fall into one of two traps. The first is to almost assume that by finishing a book, I've magically grown in some aspect of godliness. But reading something even *believing* something—isn't the same as applying it. Generally, the illusion dies quickly because temptation comes and forces me to remember that it actually takes work, not just reading, to change. My other tendency is to create unrealistic expectations of growth when feeling freshly convicted, challenged, or motivated. Then—when I realize I can't live up to these unrealistic expectations—I become paralyzed from pursuing growth at all. I want this final chapter to help you avoid those pitfalls.

## Take Steps of Obedience

Two major inhibitors to growth in godliness are delayed obedience and generic goals of change. When we feel conviction but delay obedience, the conviction inevitably fades and our hearts slowly harden. Rather than breaking old patterns, we find ways to justify them. Rather than making conscious efforts to respond to conviction, we become distracted and apathetic to the initial stirring in our hearts. In light of this, when we are challenged by Scripture or moved by the Spirit, we must immediately take steps of obedience. "When I think on my ways, I turn my feet to your testimonies; *I hasten and do not delay* to keep your commandments" (Ps. 119:59–60).

To do this, it's important to concretely define what those steps of obedience are. How many of us say that we want to read Scripture more diligently? It's a good desire, but if we fail to identify concrete ways of taking responsibility, we probably won't change. Any time I've said, "I need to work on reading my Bible," the result is typically frustration and discouragement because overly broad goals are a setup for failure. What *has* helped is asking for accountability from my husband to set my alarm earlier in order to prioritize devotional time. This creates a clear step of obedience to take the night before. Rather than praying to love God's word more and just hoping for the best, I have to consciously make the decision to set (or not set) my alarm. Far from legalism, this action of obedience is a faith-filled way to participate in God's miraculous and sanctifying work to increase my love for his word.

Likewise, if you've felt stirred to grow in generosity, establish a plan. By all means, *pray* that God makes you a cheerful giver. But then sit down, go through your budget, and determine what changes you need to make in order to live more generously. Set specific dates in your calendar to reevaluate your spending and examine whether you're growing as a generous steward or have fallen into selfish patterns. Commit to annually reading a book or listening to a sermon on generosity to refresh your vision for the mission of money.

If you have been convicted by your lack of service to the needy in your area, take some time to identify ways that you can serve and then get started. Don't wait around for God to drop something into your lap—he probably won't. Sometimes he even leads us through a process of elimination. I spent over a year volunteering at a pregnancy center, and the longer I was there, the more I felt that I was *not* a good fit and that it'd be more beneficial to serve elsewhere. However, the longer I'm involved with refugees, the more confident I am that this is where God wants me to prioritize my service. We can have faith that as we proactively obey, God will direct our steps.

## Start Dreaming

There are naïve and selfish and foolish and vain ways to dream, but there are godly ways to dream too. Even as we seek to be faithful in the small, in the ordinary, in the nothing-to-write-home-about ways, we can ask God to fill our hearts with godly ambition.

What if we started dreaming about ways to demonstrate mercy during our short life here? What if instead of dwelling on dream homes, our dream became to follow God wherever he sent us? What if instead of dreaming about accumulating money, we dreamt about ways to increase our generosity? What if instead of dedicating our saving accounts to our own comfort, we viewed them as "giving accounts" dedicated to serving God's mission? What if we adopted the mindset of Charles Wesley, who identified a modest salary to live on and pledged any additional income to kingdom endeavors? After considerable financial success, he stayed committed to this promise and, at the end of his life, had given *most* of his income away. I imagine he found far more happiness giving money away than he would have using it to enhance his lifestyle. John Piper's book royalties have amassed millions of dollars, but early into his success he decided that he wouldn't keep any of it for himself.[1] He and a board of advisors get together annually and have a wonderful time deciding how to allocate the year's royalties for the mission. Of course, most of us won't have the option of giving away millions of dollars in book royalties, but maybe we can commit to giving away bonuses, raises, overtime pay, or even our coupon savings.

What if instead of dreaming for our children's earthly success, we dreamt for their godliness? As we invest in them academically and vocationally, we can excite them to use their gifts for the sake of God's mission rather than personal ambition. There are loftier goals to pursue than financial security and career fulfillment. Almost any career can either directly or indirectly serve the ministry of mercy, so let's help our kids aspire to make the glory of God and the good of others the highest goal of their work. We can encourage them to resist the illusive search of self-fulfillment to instead find the life-giving satisfaction and happiness that come when we "seek first the kingdom of God and his righteousness" (Matt. 6:33).

So start dreaming. Make the glory of God your greatest ambition. But don't get caught up in the sparkly and spectacular. Don't chase after a sense of significance or try to conquer the world for Christ. God celebrates *faithfulness*, and faithfulness rarely

---

1 "Millions Sold, No Money Taken: What John Piper Does with His Royalties," Desiring God, October 5, 2016, https://www.desiringgod.org/.

feels inspiring. It's made up of humble choices and mundane tasks. It may not be what we romanticize, but it's real. As we fix our eyes on Christ and live each day in simple obedience and sacrifice, we'll be strengthened for future kingdom endeavors. For "one who is faithful in a very little is also faithful in much" (Luke 16:10).

## Rely on the Holy Spirit

We are utterly dependent on the Holy Spirit both for repentance and for wisdom. God doesn't leave us on our own to figure out how to please him. He's given each one of us the gift of the Holy Spirit, who illuminates Scripture to us and empowers us to apply it.

Sometimes I feel trapped in my sin and hopeless to change. But this is a lie straight from the pit of hell. Anyone found in Christ is no longer enslaved to sin. We can repent. We can change. We can become the neighbors—the doers of mercy—he's called us to be. The influence of sin remains, but its dominion has been crushed by our Savior. Now that the Spirit dwells within us, we don't have to rely on feeble self-sufficiency. The Spirit is able to overcome our fear and empower us to be bold proclaimers of the gospel, to overcome our greed and make us cheerful and generous givers, to take our eyes off the temporal and set them on the eternal. The Holy Spirit empowers the introvert to be hospitable, the cold-hearted to be compassionate, and the self-centered to be servants.

The Spirit also gives us wisdom. Scripture provides everything we need to follow Christ, for "all Scripture is breathed out by God and profitable for teaching, for reproof, for correction, and for training in righteousness, that the man of God may be complete, equipped for every good work" (2 Tim. 3:16–17). However, even as we immerse ourselves in Scripture and seek to follow its commands, we will need the wisdom of the Holy Spirit when choices are unclear.

Several years ago I contemplated multiple times whether I should quit my job in order to free up time to serve a particular ministry. When considering this, my heart was wrapped up in wanting to love my neighbor, to be a doer of mercy. However, each time I sought the Lord in prayer I felt assurance to stay at my job—for the sake of loving my neighbor. I worked with children with autism and gave portions of my income away. If I'd quit in order to free up more time to serve, I would've lost the opportunity to teach struggling children, and we would've had to decrease our giving.

All throughout our lives we are going to be faced with these types of decisions—not choices between godly and ungodly, but choices between good and good. With so many opportunities to be extenders of mercy, it's vital to prayerfully engage the Spirit about how to expend our energy and then trust him for our limitations. We are called to emulate God's heart of compassion, but we can't imitate his incommunicable attributes. We are not and never will be omnipotent, omnipresent, or omniscient and therefore aren't expected to minister in every way. Rather, we are responsible to discern where there is hardship and then prayerfully consider the specific ways God has equipped us to respond. This helps us to diligently demonstrate mercy without feeling guilty about the needs we are unable to meet.

Because of the power at work within us, we have every reason to be confident that we can grow and change. God's love has liberated us from the chains of sin and regenerated our hearts so that we can serve him.

## Prioritize Christian Community

Ever heard these types of sentiments? *Don't sit in a holy huddle— go out to reach the lost and feed the hungry! Love God, love others — nothing else matters!* They inundate social media, blogs, books, and conversations. Depending on the context, certain points might be valid, but if not engaged in deep and thoughtful ways, they won't produce healthy fruit.

Yes. Some Christians are stuck in holy huddles and desperately need to be pressed to look outward. Yet someone who only throws their life into merciful outreach at the neglect of fellowship with believers is also disobeying a crucial piece of living as a disciple. We must resist the temptation to think with an either/or mentality. Honestly, it can be *easier* to serve the needy than worry about the messiness of relationships among sinful Christians. It can be *easier* to volunteer for a nonprofit than to stay committed to a local church. But, brothers and sisters, we can't separate ourselves from a local body of believers—even the ministry of mercy is supposed to start within the family of faith, and then overflow outward (Gal. 6:10). We need the church, and the church needs us.

The Christian call to mercy is extensive and addressed far more effectively together than alone. We need to nurture relationships with other Christians who have different perspectives, strengths, and weaknesses than we do so that we can encourage one another to grow. We need to learn from one another's examples. We each have individual responsibilities, but those responsibilities are to be carried out in unity with one another. Salvation has brought us into a family—God's family—where we don't just serve him as independent individuals but together as his bride.

Being involved in a local church is critical to a faithful lifestyle of mercy. We need to be surrounded by people who stir our love for God and others. As we love God more fully, we'll be transformed more into his likeness, and the more we are transformed into his likeness, the more we will emulate his mercy.

The church is like a bonfire, and its members are like firewood. As each member participates in unity with the others, it intensifies the blaze. Any member that goes off alone is like the stray piece of wood that eventually burns out. But together—together its flames grow stronger. When the word of God ignites one of us, it spreads to those around us. Those who are ignited toward hospitality, generosity, proclamation, and service will fan others into flame. Those who emanate compassion and love justice will send out sparks that affect those around them. Those whose flames are flickering and waning will be reignited by the blazing touch of others. We need the church. It's God's most powerful way of protecting us, sanctifying us, and working through us.

The weary foster mom needs encouragement from older women whose life experiences have produced tested wisdom. The family caring for an elderly relative needs fellowship with friends who will pray for them. Those who have careers in mercy ministry need the financial support of those working nine-to-five jobs. The flock of believers who reach out to the unsaved needs the care of pastoral shepherds to guard their own walk.

There is just no way around it. Even those endeavors that we pursue individually need a body of believers that either directly or indirectly contributes. Recognizing the marriage of our personal responsibility and our need for one another prevents us from shirking our own effort and cultivates humility as we remember that we are just one part of the body and need all of its members. The church was God's design, and we are intended to work together to administer his mercy for the sake of his mission.

## Abide in Christ

Finally, as we strive to honor God in our *doing*, we must rest in what's already been *done*. Even our best deeds and holiest days are no better than rubbish if we seek our security in them. But thanks be to God—we don't rest in our own righteousness; we rest in Christ's.

Resting in Christ's righteousness allows us to experience conviction without wallowing in condemnation. It frees us to obey God with joy because we know that we don't sit under his judgment. It empowers us to strive after holiness without being chained by legalism. It is his perfect love that perfects our own.

Our union with Christ is one of the greatest miracles of salvation. If God merely forgave our past sins and provided us with a clean slate, we'd squander our second chance within moments. We'd be guilty once again. But Jesus hasn't bought us a second chance; he's imputed to us his own perfect record. He hasn't given us a temporary pardon but an eternal promise—we will stand before the judgment throne and be counted as righteous before God (Heb. 10:12–14). Where we have fallen to temptation, Jesus overcame it. Where we broke the law, he fulfilled it. Where we sacrificed others for ourselves, he sacrificed himself for the world. From his first breath on earth until his last gasp on the cross, Jesus lived a wholly righteous life. When God looks at us, he no longer sees our sins and shortcomings. He sees his Son's obedience. Though we may neglect our neighbors and fail to show mercy, he never does.

This book was meant to be practical—actionable. It's meant to help you *go* and *do*. But our doing will go wrong if it keeps us from abiding. In our efforts to live for Jesus we can drift from communing with Jesus. Consider the story of Mary and Martha (Luke 10:38–42). Martha loved Jesus. She joyfully welcomed him into her home and busied herself to serve him. She wasn't being selfish with her time at all. But stressed and resentful, she complained to Jesus that Mary sat at his feet instead of helping. She saw her service to the Lord as more important than being with the Lord. Jesus kindly reminded her, "Martha, Martha, you are anxious and troubled about many things, but one thing is necessary. Mary has chosen the good portion, which will not be taken away from her" (Luke 10:41–42).

Our deeds cannot overshadow our devotion. Service *to* Jesus must always be the overflow of love *for* Jesus. "We love because he first loved us" (1 John 4:19). God revealed himself in Scripture so that we can know and love and serve him. He wants us to seek him, to commune with him. And the more we abide and find our fullness in him, the more we can pour ourselves out in mercy to others.

## Discussion Questions

1. What are some practical steps of obedience you plan to take to "go and do likewise"? How can you seek accountability to take those steps?

2. What are some dreams you have for the future? How are they related to love of God and neighbor?

3. How can you cultivate a greater dependence on the Holy Spirit as you seek to grow in mercy?

4. Why is local church involvement and community so essential to sustaining a lifestyle of mercy? In what ways are you pursuing this kind of fellowship?

5. Read John 15:4–5. What does it mean to abide in Christ?

# Acknowledgments

I ACTUALLY WROTE the first draft of this book in 2015. It was twice as long, and, honestly, it was pretty terrible. I'm so grateful for the many people who saw it in its early, messy, undeveloped stages and played a part in refining it.

Andrew, this book truly wouldn't exist without you. You took my writing seriously even before I did. I'm so grateful for your unwavering support and relentless encouragement. It's such a privilege to be loved by you. Isaac, Reed, and Tulasi, I love you and am so proud of the way you care for others.

Mom, you exemplify what it means to love big while faithfully pursuing ministry in the mundane. Thank you for advocating for this book, even when I wanted to give up on it. Dad, I'll never forget sitting in your office as you went through my manuscript line by line and gave me such specific encouragement and insightful feedback. Thank you for always reminding me to keep Christ central. Jeff, thanks for pushing me to pursue publishing back when I thought it was just a pipe dream.

To my friends, fellow writers, and first readers: Katie Faris, Laurie Reyes, Jamie Finn, and Andy Farmer. Katie, thank you for helping me discern the book's strengths and weaknesses—your notes were so helpful. Laurie, thank you for your enthusiasm when I sheepishly handed you my "book baby"—it was the reassurance I needed. Jamie, thank you for sharing this passion, living by example, and being my sounding board. Andy, thank you for your timely guidance and support.

To my church family. Thank you for all the ways you reflect God's mercy and live as a light in South Jersey. It's an honor to follow Christ with you.

To the team at Crossway, you work with excellence, and it's a joy to partner with you. Todd, your enthusiasm behind this project meant so much. Samuel, your discerning eye was profoundly helpful. Lydia, I'm so grateful for your hard work to edit and improve this book—hopefully someday I'll learn to keep my exclamation points in check!

Finally, to my Savior, thank you for your great love, mercy, and compassion. You are a good and gracious King—it's such a comfort to trust that someday you will mend everything that is broken.

Appendix

# How Can I Discern Which Organization to Support?

RATHER THAN HAVING a cut-and-dried approach to what makes a "good" ministry, it's important to identify the nuanced reasons that some are more effective (physically and/or spiritually) than others. Fruitfulness will manifest differently for a medical outreach organization working in a war zone and a prison ministry working in the city. Stewardship will look different for an organization that provides food for orphans (where money stretches far) and one that provides legal aid for immigrants (where processes are expensive). To help us discern worthy para church ministries and charitable organizations to support, we should take three basic factors into consideration: fruitfulness of approach, integrity of people, and stewardship of finances. My friend and pastor Scott Faris, who has spent decades working in various ministry and nonprofit positions, created the following excellent outline of questions.

*Fruitfulness of Approach*

- How do they learn from and respond to their mistakes at home or in the field?
- Does their work represent a sound understanding of context and need for those they serve?
- What is unique about how they, as an organization, have been gifted and called to serve? Are they being faithful to steward those distinctive opportunities?
- Does the organization reflect biblical values in how it works with indigenous populations and partners as colaborers?
- How would they define the fruit of their endeavors in light of following the Spirit's leading?
- Does the organization embrace sound doctrine?

*Integrity of People*

- What is the overall "temperature" of the work environment at headquarters and in the field?
- Have there been any major scandals involving leadership or staff that are credible?
- How did the organization deal with any scandals?
- How are decisions made, and what impact have organizational decisions had on workers and beneficiaries?
- Do members/workers in this organization have a clear sense of and adherence to standards of transparency?
- How are grievances handled when they are brought to the attention of leadership?
- Are the people who work for the organization Christians?

- What standards of conduct are employees and volunteers held to, and does that change place to place?
- If the organization has a strong central leader, how have others been utilized and empowered to serve and lead?
- If certain high-profile staff were to leave the organization, could it endure that change?

*Stewardship of Finances*

- Does the board of directors have actual power to lead the organization, or does it act more as a rubber stamp for a founding leader or leaders?
- Do family members involved with the ministry have adequate checks and balances to their decisions, especially financial ones?
- Are all financial transactions recorded by standard accounting practices and then audited and/or made available to both the board and donors?
- When money is given to an organization, can donors easily find out how it was used?
- Is there any history of financial discrepancies or malpractice in the organization's history? If so, what changes were made in the wake of those challenges?
- Who gives money to this organization, and why? What are their reasons for investing in its work?

Don't try to answer all of these questions at once or wait to find a flawless organization (they don't exist!) before you give. Be intentional over time, start giving, and pray for discernment to make changes when necessary.

# Recommended Reading

Anyabwile, Thabiti. *The Gospel for Muslims: An Encouragement to Share Christ with Confidence*. Chicago: Moody, 2010.

Alcorn, Randy. *Managing God's Money: A Biblical Guide*. Carol Stream, IL: Tyndale, 2011.

————. *The Treasure Principle: Unlocking the Secret of Joyful Giving*. Revised Edition. Colorado Springs, CO: Multnomah, 2017.

Bauman, Stephan, Matthew Soerens, and Issam Smeir. *Seeking Refuge: On the Shores of the Global Refugee Crisis*. Chicago: Moody, 2016.

Darling, Daniel. *The Dignity Revolution: Reclaiming God's Rich Vision for Humanity*. Charlotte, NC: Good Book Company, 2018.

Finn, Jamie. *Foster the Family: Encouragement, Hope, and Practical Help for the Christian Foster Parent*. Grand Rapids, MI: Baker, 2022.

Johnson, Andy. *Missions: How the Local Church Goes Global*. Wheaton, IL: Crossway, 2017.

Keller, Timothy. *Generous Justice: How God's Grace Makes Us Just*. New York: Penguin, 2016.

————. *Ministries of Mercy: The Call of the Jericho Road*. Phillipsburg, NJ: P&R, 2015.

Lacey, Carolyn. *Extraordinary Hospitality (for Ordinary People): Sevens Ways to Welcome Like Jesus*. Charlotte, NC: Good Book Company, 2021.

Moore, Russell. *Adopted for Life: The Priority of Adoption for Christian Families and Churches*. Wheaton, IL: Crossway, 2009.

Platt, David. *Follow Me: A Call to Die, a Call to Live*. Carol Stream, IL: Tyndale, 2013.

———. *Radical: Taking Back Your Faith from the American Dream*. Colorado Springs, CO: Multnomah, 2010.

# General Index

# Scripture Index

# Also Available from Amy DiMarcangelo

This book invites readers to feast at the table of grace, where they will find God's vast glory and his intimate care, his strength made perfect in weakness, and his gifts of joy and comfort to his children—that they "may be filled with all the fullness of God."

For more information, visit **crossway.org**.